F E Cerruti, Eusebio de Salazar y Mazarredo

Peru and Spain

Being a narrative of the events preceding and following the seizure of the Chincha Islands, with an analysis of the despatch of Señor Salazar y Mazarredo

F E Cerruti, Eusebio de Salazar y Mazarredo

Peru and Spain

Being a narrative of the events preceding and following the seizure of the Chincha Islands, with an analysis of the despatch of Señor Salazar y Mazarredo

ISBN/EAN: 9783337246143

Printed in Europe, USA, Canada, Australia, Japan

Cover: Foto ©ninafisch / pixelio.de

More available books at **www.hansebooks.com**

PERU AND SPAIN,

BEING

A NARRATIVE OF THE EVENTS

PRECEDING AND FOLLOWING THE

SEIZURE OF THE CHINCHA ISLANDS,

WITH

AN ANALYSIS OF THE DESPATCH

OF

SEÑOR SALAZAR Y MAZARREDO,

HER CATHOLIC MAJESTY'S "SPECIAL COMMISSARY" TO PERU,
AND MINISTER TO BOLIVIA,

DETAILING

HIS ADVENTUROUS VOYAGE HOMEWARDS.

By CAPTAIN F. E. CERRUTI,

Ex-Private Secretary to H.C.M.'s "Special Commissary."

WILLIAMS AND NORGATE,
14, HENRIETTA STREET, COVENT GARDEN, LONDON;
AND 20, SOUTH FREDERICK STREET, EDINBURGH.
1864.

CONTENTS.

	PAGE.
DEDICATORY LETTER . . .	1
INTRODUCTORY REMARKS	3
PART FIRST:—	5

THE ORIGIN OF THE DIFFICULTY BETWEEN PERU AND SPAIN.
THE CAPTURE OF THE CHINCHA ISLANDS.
OFFICIAL CORRESPONDENCE.

PART SECOND:— 38

THE VOYAGE HOME. PERSONAL ADVENTURES.
ANALYSIS OF SEÑOR SALAZAR Y MAZARREDO'S DESPATCH.

POSTSCRIPT 57

APPENDIX 61

I. EXTRACT OF CIRCULAR OF SEÑOR PACHECO, ACCOMPANYING THE DESPATCH OF SEÑOR SALAZAR Y MAZARREDO 61

II. COPIES OF CIRCULARS FROM THE SOUTH AMERICAN REPUBLICS, ON RECEIPT OF INTELLIGENCE OF THE SEIZURE OF THE CHINCHA ISLANDS . 63

III. BRIEF ACCOUNT OF THE CHINCHAS AND OTHER "GUANO" ISLANDS 71

DEDICATORY LETTER.

London, 1*st September*, 1864.

To the Señores Caballeros
    Luis de Cepeda y Granados,
    Antonio Cencio y Romero,
    Melchor Ordoñez y Ortega,
    Fernando Ordoñez y Ortega.

Esteemed Friends,

    I am so greatly indebted to you for innumerable acts of kindness shown to me during the many months we were together, that I feel a singular pleasure in thus connecting your names with a production of my pen. I might have hesitated to do so in respect of a more imposing work, but I am confident that the liberty I take will be easily pardoned me on this occasion, when I assure you that the present pamphlet is written with a view to facilitate the return to a better understanding between Peru and Spain, by explaining away the chief causes of the hostile attitude assumed by the latter country towards one of her fairest daughters.

    I know you to be all brave and generous. I know you would freely sacrifice your lives for the good of your glorious land; but I fear to see you fall in what, I cannot but think an unworthy cause, if you should become the victims of a war generated from ignoble motives, and fanned into flame by unscrupulous instruments.

    Understand me rightly. I do not by the latter term allude to the Admiral now in command of your country's squadron in the Pacific. I believe him to be an upright gentleman and gallant officer, who, incapable of meanness himself, is too apt to believe in the honour of others. I refer more especially to the man, who, having it in his power to conciliate differences which he was actually commissioned to settle, has chosen rather to increase them, and who, to soothe his wounded self-love or gratify some malignant feeling, has not hesitated to resort to measures which will, I sincerely hope, be yet turned against their author.

Trusting in all sincerity that under the leadership of the gallant Pinzon, you will acquire that noble fame to which your aspirations tend,

I respectfully subscribe myself,
Esteemed Friends,
Your hearty well-wisher,
F. E. C.

41, *Museum Street*,
 Bloomsbury.

PERU AND SPAIN.

INTRODUCTORY REMARKS.

A CAREFUL examination of the Circular addressed on the 24th June last by H. E. Señor J. F. Pacheco, Minister of State of Her Catholic Majesty to the representatives of Spain abroad, and by them laid before the Governments to which they are respectively accredited, has led me to believe that if the true history of the Spanish-Peruvian difficulty were better known in Spain and elsewhere, it would go far towards preventing the having recourse to hostilities.

Moved by this conviction and possessed of an intimate knowledge of the events preceding and following the seizure of the Chincha Islands; being also fully aware of the degree of credit to be given to the "Special Commissary's" despatch, which is appended to Señor Pacheco's Circular, I propose to lay before my readers a true and impartial statement of the events which led to the rupture between the two Governments, in the hope that it may do something towards the prevention of a war, which, once begun, would extend to a great part of the South American Continent, for there is little doubt but that the other Republics would make common cause with Peru, if Spain should be so ill-advised as to prosecute this quarrel to its threatened end.

As Señor Pacheco intimates that peace is impossible unless the Peruvian Government shall, "by satisfactory explanations and protestations of innocence," remove from herself the suspicious cast upon her by Señor Salazar's despatch, as he considers that the grievances therein detailed "eclipse all others which Spain conceives that she has against Peru," I intend (having in my capacity of Señor Salazar's private Secretary, been his fellow-traveller from Callao to Southampton), to place in a proper light the grave accusations which the Spanish Special Commissary has brought against the Peruvian Government. I am prompted to do this, not only as a friend of peace, but as one revolting against the perversion of honest truth, and from that feeling which, when gratuitous insult is added to injury, "makes every man of spirit a partisan." While doing so, however, I am conscious that an adherence to the strictest truth will be my solemn duty, and that by such a course I shall be most likely to succeed in smothering that unholy feeling which the artful despatch of Señor Salazar has excited, and which is now smouldering in the breasts of two kindred nations; creating at present the chief obstacle to a settlement of their differences.

In dealing with this document as I propose to do, paragraph by paragraph, I shall give it translated into English, with such comments as in my character of an eye-witness, I am in a position to append. I consider it my duty to dwell thus, at length, upon this production of Señor Salazar y Mazarredo, because the charges which he brings against Peru are of such a nature as to preclude the probability that a Government — acknowledged by Señor Pacheco to be an enlightened one—will deign to exonerate itself of calumnies which redound, not to the disadvantage of the accused, but to the shame and confusion of the unscrupulous accuser. It remains, therefore, for those whose knowledge gives them a right to speak upon the subject, freely to place in possession of the public the necessary data to form an opinion.

Having thus defined my position and the motives which have induced me to come forward at this juncture, I shall, with the reader's permission, proceed to my self-allotted task.

PART FIRST.

THE ORIGIN OF THE DIFFICULTY BETWEEN PERU AND SPAIN.—THE SEIZURE OF THE CHINCHA ISLANDS.

In the month of November, 1863, there arrived at Panamá the "Bolivia," one of the Steamers of the Pacific Mail Steam Navigation Company, bringing the news of a conflict which had taken place at Talambo, an insignificant Peruvian hamlet, wherein some Spaniards had lost their lives, and others had been seriously wounded.

On the receipt of this intelligence, Admiral Pinzon, in command of the Spanish force in the Pacific, and then at Panamá, resolved to forego an intended cruise to Guayaquil and sail at once for Callao, with the object of inquiring into the matter.

Propelled by steam, the "Resolucion," (the Spanish flag-ship), reached that port on the 14th December, and on the following day the Admiral, having hired a residence at Lima, entered into communication with the Peruvian authorities for the purpose of obtaining the punishment of the guilty parties in the affair of Talambo.

For the information of my readers, I must here digress to inform them that Talambo is little more than a large farm in the northern part of Peru, the exclusive property of Señor Manuel Salcedo, a wealthy and educated gentleman, who, desiring to improve the immense tracts of land which had for ages remained untilled, owing to the want of hands, sent agents to Spain to invite over a large number of colonists for the purpose of cultivating cotton on his estates. On the arrival of Señor Salcedo's envoys in the old country, they engaged some seventy families who agreed to emigrate, providing their expenses were paid—a condition which was faithfully performed.

While the preparations for the departure of the future colonists were making, the matter came to the ears of the Spanish Government who, to the emigrants' astonishment, opposed their departure —presumably on the ground that it was derogatory to the lofty character of the nation, that her subjects should be hired as colonists. This opposition, however, served no other end than to induce the emigrants to seek a foreign port of departure, which they found in France, whence, with French passports, they embarked for Callao, on board a vessel chartered by Señor Salcedo, who not only defrayed the expenses of the passage but advanced moneys to several of the colonists to provide them with a proper outfit.

On arriving at Callao, some of these men broke faith with their employer, and engaged themselves and families to other parties without so much as an attempt to reimburse the sums advanced on their behalf. The greater part, however, proceeded to Talambo, where by their assiduity to labour and general good conduct they secured the esteem of their master and gathered comforts about their homes.

Things went on thus prosperously till the 4th August 1863, when, a dispute having arisen between some of the Peruvian labourers and a number of the Spanish colonists, one of the latter was killed and four were wounded: the casualties on the other side being one man killed and five wounded. The total number of persons engaged in this affair did not exceed forty, and the assertion of Señor Salazar, that *seventy armed* Peruvians fell upon *eighteen unarmed* Spaniards, is perfectly unfounded, nor can a single declaration of a reliable person be brought forward to substantiate it. Nor can the assertion of Señor Salazar that the affair was a premeditated one, having for object the extirpation of the Spanish colonists, and that the authorities were not only parties to it but actually sent some of their menials to assist in the unholy work, be regarded as worthy of credence; for if this were the fact, what was there to prevent the colonists being slaughtered to a man? Surely not the *eighteen unarmed* Spaniards treacherously taken unawares by *seventy* blood-thirsty assassins! But it is useless to argue such a point. I repeat, and intelligent persons will surely coincide with me, that the riot was purely accidental, and that the parties engaged in it were about equally divided, as the casualties will prove;—but that in no case can the Government of Peru be responsible for an event which was just as likely to arise in the old world as the new; under the oldest as the youngest dynasties. That the Government was not, however, indifferent to the matter is shown by the course taken by the authorities, who no sooner heard of the affair than they took all constitutional means to bring the guilty parties to justice.

It may be, that the energy with which the matter was taken up was not due to a sense of justice only. It is possible that a desire to maintain a good understanding with Spain and to prevent this untoward affair being used, by unscrupulous men in that country, as a pretext for fresh charges and accusations against Peru, had its weight in inducing the Government to exert itself towards obtaining a prompt and impartial administration of the laws. But, however great might be the wish of the authorities to bring the matter to a speedy and favourable issue, they could do no more than compel the attendance of witnesses and employ able counsel in the case;—the rest remained with the Tribunal itself;—and it was while the cause was still pending in the Court to whose jurisdiction it was submitted that the events occurred which we shall describe hereafter.

This Talambo brawl,—for it deserves no higher title,—is put forward by Señor Salazar as a *casus belli*. So important in his eyes is this squabble between a handful of irresponsible persons that he uses it as an excuse to kidnap various civil and military officers of a State with which his country is at peace, to confiscate its treasures, and—what is even perhaps more unpardonable still, —to brand the entire nation with perfidy, and declare their judges wholly unfit to administer justice.

I now return to Admiral Pinzon, who, on his arrival at Lima, was received with all the honours due to so distinguished a guest. His reception at the capital was in fact a brilliant one, and during his stay a round of entertainments indicated the desire of the people to maintain friendly relations with the country he represented. The same demonstrations followed him to the coast, and not to be behindhand in civility, the Admiral, on his return to Callao, gave a banquet and ball on board of the flag-ship, which were graced by the presence of many noble ladies and the élite of Peruvian society.

There is no doubt that, prior to his coming in contact with Señor Salazar, Admiral Pinzon acted with good faith towards the Peruvians. He had come to inquire into the affair of Talambo. He had presumably received satisfactory explanations. These entertainments mutually given and accepted are proof of this position, and a further evidence of such a view is afforded by the fact, that when he left Callao in March of the present year, he had resolved to take his fleet to Spain.

I say *resolved* advisedly, although such intention was not communicated to me in words. My conclusions were drawn from what I there saw passing beneath my eyes. As thus:—At Valparaiso, where the vessels made some stay, I observed officers and sailors purchasing winter clothing, which would be of little use to them if remaining in Peru, although indispensable in a passage round Cape Horn. I remarked that the old sails were removed and new ones bent; a customary precaution even among merchant vessels, when about to leave those latitudes for the more stormy ones of the Cape. And I noticed that the vessels were thoroughly overhauled and caulked, as if to prepare them for a long and trying voyage.

If further evidence were necessary of the intended destination of the fleet, it would be found in the great surprise felt and expressed by all on board, when, on the 29th of March, orders were given to remove the new sails and replace the old ones; a surprise that grew into astonishment, when it became known that the Admiral had received instructions to take in a full complement of powder, and return immediately to Callao.

As these instructions reached Valparaiso on the 29th of March, or probably the day before, it is reasonable to suppose that it was written before the 20th of that month; and if this be so, it becomes unnecessary to assert that the intentions of Señor Salazar y Mazarredo were hostile, when he arrived at Lima. It is therefore very presumable, that if Señor Ribeyro, the Peruvian Minister for Foreign Affairs, had admitted him to his council, so far from any good result being obtained, the pretensions of the envoy would rather have increased the existing difficulties.

The fleet being thus prepared for all contingencies, the Admiral sailed from Valparaiso on the 7th of April, on board the "Resolucion;" the frigate "Triunfo" following close behind.

On the 14th of April, at 10·30 A.M. the fleet being at the time within some six miles of the Chincha Islands, we sighted the Spanish sloop of war "Covadonga," having on board Señor Salazar y Mazarredo. On drawing nearer, a boat was lowered from the latter vessel into which the envoy descended, and who was so childishly anxious to communicate the intelligence with which he was bursting, that he stood up in the gig as it approached the flag-ship, and shouted out to those on board to go and tell the Admiral that "they had refused to receive him." Two minutes afterwards, he came up the side and in an excited manner explained to the Admiral that the Peruvians had refused to grant him an audience. The result of their conversation was an order to have the vessels prepared for action!

Everything being in readiness, the vessels stood in shore, and with almost as little delay as it takes to write it, the Governor was summoned to surrender the Islands, and a like peremptory message was conveyed to the Commander of the "Iquique," a Peruvian vessel of war, lying at anchor in the roadstead.

The hurried nature of these most extraordinary proceedings, may be gathered from the following letters, exchanged between Admiral Pinzon and Ramon Valle-Riestra, the Governor of the Chincha Islands, and which, incredible as it may seem, formed the only correspondence that preceded an act, as barefaced and unscrupulous as any of those perpetrated by Spanish commanders in the same seas, centuries before.

Admiral Pinzon to the Governor of the Chincha Islands.

"Anchorage of the Chinchas, April 14th, 1864.

"Being determined to take possession of the Chincha Islands by means of the force under my command, I communicate this to you, that you may deliver them up to me; if you do not I shall take them by main force.

God preserve, &c.
(*signed*) LUIZ H. PINZON."

Reply of the Governor of the Chincha Islands to the Vice-Admiral of the Spanish squadron.

"Administration of the Chincha Islands, April 14th, 1864.

"I have received the note of this day's date, which the Admiral has been pleased to address to me, in which he calls upon me to place these Islands at his disposal, and says that in case of my not doing so he will take possession of them by force. I now have to inform the Admiral in reply, that I have no instructions from my Government on this matter, and, therefore, not being able to act in an affair of such importance, I will ask for the necessary instructions, hoping that the Admiral will be pleased to allow me the time necessary to receive them.

I have, &c.
(*signed*) RAMON VALLE-RIESTRA.

Admiral Pinzon to the Governor of the Chincha Islands.

"Anchorage of the Chinchas, April 14th, 1864.

"In reply to your polite note which I have just received, I inform you that the Naval Ensign who brings this communication carries a Spanish flag, which he will substitute for that of the Republic of Peru within fifteen minutes without delay. If this be not done, he will immediately open fire without any further consideration, and you will be responsible for the blood which may be shed and the property destroyed.

God preserve, &c.
(*signed*) LUIZ H. PINZON."

Reply of the Governor of the Chincha Islands to the Vice-Admiral of the Spanish squadron.

"Administration of the Chincha Islands, April 14th, 1864.

"SIR,

"I have in my hands the Admiral's second note of this day's date, in which he refuses to give me the time necessary for receiving instructions from my Government upon the notice which he has sent to me to deliver up these islands to him and he repeats that notice. I reply to that note by saying to the Admiral, that being without instructions, as I have stated, it is not in my power to surrender them; but if the Admiral, making use of the large force under his command, shall carry into effect the act which he proposes, I shall protest, as I do now protest, in the name of the Supreme Government of the Republic, against the violence which the Spanish vessels, now at anchor in the port, exercise against Peru, and that the Admiral will be responsible for the consequences which his act may draw upon the people, as also for the

damage that may be caused to foreign vessels which are now loading.
I am, &c.
(*signed*) RAMON VALLE-RIESTRA."

On the receipt of this last letter, the Admiral perceived that it was necessary to employ force to obtain possession of the coveted prize, and he therefore ordered troops to be landed under the command of Señor Don José Caudenes, a naval ensign of great determination, who fulfilled to the letter the commission intrusted to him.

Although I was a spectator of the entire occurrence I prefer giving a description of the event in the words of Mr. John Dartnell, Her Britannic Majesty's Vice-Consul at Pisco, who, from the fact of his being a disinterested spectator of the proceedings, may perhaps be listened to with more complete confidence than a person whom circumstances compelled to take an active share in the scenes he describes.

Vice Consul Dartnell to Mr. Jerningham.
"Chincha Islands, April 13*th*, 1864.

" SIR,
Yesterday, about 10 or 11 o'clock a.m., a Spanish steamer of war hove in sight from the north, and presently she was seen to be signalising with two vessels from the south, that eventually proved to be Spanish steam-frigates of war. Shortly afterwards an officer from the Admiral's ship came on shore with despatches for the Governor of these islands, and in a few minutes he retired, when it became known that the possession of these islands was demanded within the space of a few hours.

The Governor, in answer to the demands of the Spanish authorities, refused to deliver up the islands or haul down the Peruvian flag without orders from his Government; but not having a sufficient force to defend the place, and attend to the security of the large number of convicts here at work in the guano, and also being desirous of avoiding useless bloodshed, he had to allow the Spanish force to come unmolested on shore, and proceed as their judgment advised. He, the Governor, being powerless, had only to protest in the most formal manner.

Somewhere about half past 3 p.m. an armed force in several boats was seen to proceed from the Spanish fleet on board the Peruvian vessel of war "Iquique," when presently her flag was hauled down and the Spanish ensign hoisted at the peak.

Immediately afterwards the same body of men (about 400, more or less) proceeded on shore, and straightway took possession of the Government House, and hoisted the Spanish flag, when a salute of twenty-one guns was fired by the before-mentioned vessels of war.

Soon after this I was honoured with a visit from Señor Salazar y Mazarredo, the Spanish Commissary or Minister, who assured me that both he and Admiral Pinzon would guarantee the security of all property, both foreign and Peruvian, on the islands, and that in no way should the loading of the vessels be interfered with, and that after loading they could proceed to Callao as usual.

On the retiring from the islands of the Admiral, Señor Mazarredo, and the Spanish troops, the Governor, Señor Captain Don Ramon Valle-Riestra, the Captain of the Port, Señor Captain Don Diego de la Haza, and the Commander of the "Iquique," Señor Captain Don Augustin Ariolo, were taken on board the flag-ship in character of prisoners; and up to the present none of these gentlemen have returned on shore, so I suppose they must have proceeded on to Callao in the fleet.

The officers and crew of the "Iquique" have also been taken away, and only some ten or twelve men from the Spanish men-of-war left on board, with, it is said, orders not to communicate with the islands.

On shore we are completely abandoned, for not a single Peruvian soldier was left here, the "guarnicion," together with the convicts, having been taken off the islands, and sent, I believe, to Pisco in a Peruvian vessel of commerce which sailed last night.

Owing to the state of abandon in which this place has been left, the greatest alarm was felt last night and still continues to be felt; but owing to the exertions of some persons here, headed and encouraged by the Cargador, Señor Calderon, a guard has been formed, and the streets during the night are to be patrolled. Nevertheless, as this population is formed of some of the worst kind of characters, and as the British Vice-Consulate is actually the deposit of considerable money and property belonging to several persons here, I do not feel altogether at ease, and should really, as well as others here, wish to see the flag of even the smallest British vessel of war in our harbour.

When, Sir, you consider that at this moment there is not one single employé of the Peruvian Government, much less of the Spanish, on these islands, I hope that you will take into consideration my position, and, if possible, send a vessel of war here, so that the minds of the British subjects here be set at rest, and that in case of a riot we may know where and how to apply for protection.

Thinking it my duty to apprize you as quickly as possible of what has taken place here,

I have, &c.
(*signed*) JOHN DARTNELL."

Thus runs the official account of this notable transaction. There are minor points of interest which that statement naturally does not touch (but that are still useful to make the picture complete), and I therefore supply them for the information of my readers.

Prior to the arrival of the steam-frigates "Resolucion" and "Triunfo," the "Covadonga" (with Señor Salazar on board) commanded by Señor Luis Fery, had been behaving herself in a way which proved pretty clearly the disposition that was felt to conduct matters with a high hand.

After ordering an English merchant vessel bound for Callao to heave to, and forbidding her master to proceed on his voyage without permission, she captured three small schooners engaged in carrying provisions to the Islands, and would have held them as lawful prizes, but for the interposition of Captain Emanuel de la Rigada, the worthy commander of the "Resolucion," who, declaring them to be seized contrary to the established usages of civilized warfare, ordered them to be at once set free.

With regard to the sloop "Iquique;" captured in the way narrated by Mr. Dartnell, I may mention that she is nothing more than a small schooner, barque-rigged, of about 200 tons burthen, whose full complement of sailors, officers, and soldiers does not exceed sixty men, all told. My attention was more particularly called to her by a remark made by the chief mate of a vessel that was loading guano, on board of which I happened to be some few days after the events above narrated.

"Do the Spaniards now, mean to do what's right in Peru?" inquired the man.

"Oh, yes; I should hope so," was my answer.

"Well; I'm glad of that any how," he rejoined. "There's nothing like a good beginning at all events. Everything that's begun well, ends well:—so you can tell the Admiral he may return me the 'Iquique.' The Peruvians took her from me because they caught me stealing guano. It is my opinion she'll never bring any luck to her owners. She hasn't thus far, at all events; for she's only gone from the hands of one thief into those of another."

I could not withhold a laugh at the cool impudence of the speaker; but I felt too little confidence in the motives which had actuated the leaders in the transactions that had just transpired to hazard any observation in reply, so turned upon my heel.

As Mr. Dartnell, in his note to Mr. Jerningham, only briefly alludes to the march of the invaders to the Government House, it may not be amiss to mention the manner of the Governor's capture, which occurred as follows:—On the refusal of Captain Ramon Valle-Riestra to surrender the place, between three and four hundred men were disembarked from the fleet in ten large boats,—four of them armed with artillery,—and on reaching the shore, they proceeded in martial order, a band of music playing and colours flying, to the Governor's house.

When the heads of the party were introduced into the presence of the Governor, Admiral Pinzon, with all the urbanity of manner inherent to his nature, desired that gentleman to surrender his sword; which request being complied with, the Admiral began politely to converse with the discomfited official, and put him, as far as circumstances would allow, at his ease. Not so Salazar, the prime mover of this audacious enterprize, who, although silent throughout the interview, betrayed by his look and demeanour a degree of irritability that he had much ado to restrain.

A close observer of Señor Salazar's behaviour on this occasion, attributes his ill-humour to the following incident:

While, with an assumption of nonchalance, he cast his eyes about the room, his attention was caught by a picture hanging on the wall, which, on examination, he found to bear this inscription:

"Illmo Señor—Tempus breve est, et debemus sitere ante Tribunal Domini, ut redeamus rationem omnibus operibus nostris, et in speciali de injusticiis adversus proximos nostros."

If our "Special Commissary" had not become quite callous, it is possible that such a very home-thrust did awaken some uncomfortable reflections in his mind.

The capture of the Chinchas being thus effected, it will not be out of place to examine a little into the circumstances which immediately led to it, for my readers must not be left to imagine that such a high-handed measure was the result of the Talambo riot. Oh, no; the *recovery* of the Guano Islands was undertaken and brought to the issue we have described in order to avenge an offence of far deeper dye. It was determined on for the purpose of punishing the Peruvian nation for their want of courtesy towards Señor Don Eusebio Salazar y Mazarredo, Special Commissary of Her Catholic Majesty, Queen Isabella II.

The official correspondence, which I annex, puts this matter in a clear light, and I shall content myself with simply adding to it, as I go on, a few remarks where explanations may appear necessary.

Her Britannic Majesty's Chargé d'Affaires, writing to Earl Russell from Lima on the 13th April, 1864, respecting this Peruvian question, makes the following statement:—

"Señor Salazar, having presented his credentials to the Peruvian Minister for Foreign Affairs, the latter returned for answer, according to the document, copy of which I beg to annex, that the Peruvian Government would be happy to receive him, and give him those facilities and means which the law allows for the accomplishment of his mission, and that as the letter of the 18th of January accredited Señor Salazar y Mazarredo in purely a confidential character, they accept him as invested with such: but that, at the same time, they cannot agree to the denomination of Commissary, as this would be at variance with the diplomatic rules and usages, and give rise to embarrassments in the course of negotiations, concluding that if Señor Salazar agreed to this understanding, the Peruvian Minister informs him that he might commence his mission when he thought proper."

After alluding to the puerile and discourteous reply of Señor Salazar, the honourable gentleman concludes with the following remarks, which show very clearly the bent of his opinion:

"This is the unforeseen termination of Señor Mazarredo's mission; and I think it is the more to be regretted, as, up to the time of the Talambo difficulty, there has not been in this Republic any general or real animosity against Spaniards or Spain; in proof of which there are many rich and influential Spaniards resident in Peru who have made fortunes here, and who have not met, apparently, I should imagine, with impediments and vexations either in their commercial or social careers, on account of their nationality.

(signed)   WM. STAFFORD JERNINGHAM."

The extracts I have just quoted show conclusively that Señor Salazar was met with all courtesy by the authorities of Peru, who at once expressed their readiness to open negotiations with him on a footing which should be intelligible, and which his very title defined. The mendacity of Señor Salazar, in stating that he was refused admission, is on a par with the arrogance which has marked his conduct throughout the whole of these disgraceful proceedings.

It is difficult to conceive the motive of Señor Salazar's refusal of the Peruvian Minister's proposal to accept him in the capacity of a confidential agent, unless it is explained by a pre-determination *not* to carry out the mission of peace with which he was presumably entrusted.

That Señor Ribeyro was justified in viewing Señor Salazar in a confidential capacity, will be shown by the wording of his credentials, which I transcribe; and the temperate and gentlemanly communications of Señor Ribeyro—which I likewise annex—will prove that the Peruvian Minister was animated with the best desire to have a proper understanding with the government of the mother-country.

Señor Arrazola, Chief Secretary of State of H. C. M. to Señor Ribeyro, Minister for Foreign Affairs of Peru.

"Madrid, January 18, 1864.

"SIR,
"Thinking it conducive to the interests of Spain in her relations with Peru, to send to that Republic a Special Commissary, who by his experience and personal qualities, should be able to draw closer the ties which ought to unite the two States, and the

requisite conditions being found united in Don Eusebio de Salazar y Mazarredo, Deputy to the Cortes, and late Political Sub-Director in the Ministry of State, I request that your Excellency will be pleased to acknowledge him as such Special Commissary, and to pay attention to him in regard to the business with which he is charged.

"At the same time, I beg that your Excellency will be pleased to receive the Caballero de Salazar y Mazarredo favourably, and in the meanwhile, I avail, &c.

(signed)   LORENZO ARRAZOLA."

Señor Ribeyro to Señor Salazar y Mazarredo.

"Lima, April 1, 1864.

"The Government of Peru, faithful interpreter of the public feeling, is always ready to distinguish itself in its international relations by acts of loyalty and goodwill. Guided by the principles of this frank policy, it will receive Señor de Salazar y Mazarredo, deputed to this Ministry by his Excellency the President of the Council and Chief Secretary of State to Her Catholic Majesty, with the most lively cordiality, giving him those facilities, and conceding to him all those privileges which the law recognizes, and which are necessary for the faithful discharge of his commission.

"As the communication of the 18th of January of the present year, accredits Señor de Salazar in a purely confidential character, to judge from its context, the Cabinet of the undersigned Minister of Foreign Affairs, accepts him at once as such Agent of the Cabinet of Madrid, because the denomination of Commissary, on account of its not being in conformity with diplomatic rules and usages, might lead perhaps to embarrassments in the course of the negotiations, which, for the good of both Governments, ought to be prevented at any cost. If Señor Salazar admits, as it is to be hoped he will, this preliminary and necessary explanation, he can enter upon his mission whenever he may think fit, secure of meeting, on the part of Peru and its Administration, with the most happy dispositions to come to a good understanding with the Representative of the enlightened Spanish nation.

"With sentiments, &c.
(signed)   JUAN ANTO. RIBEYRO."

The foregoing letter needs little comment. It is urbane—even friendly. The Peruvian Minister, construing the title of "Special Commissary," as that of a "Confidential Agent," frankly admits him in that character, and assures him that whilst he can commence his mission without delay, he shall receive every facility and courtesy in carrying it out.

Twelve days elapsed from its receipt, before the Special Commissary made any sign, and when he at last did so, it was to fling back one of the most extraordinary communications ever emanating from a diplomatic personage. He seems himself to have feared the consequences of his coarse and insulting epistle, for no sooner was it despatched, than the "Covadonga," upon which he had embarked, stood out to sea.

The singular effusion to which I have alluded, is thus conceived:

Señor Salazar y Mazarredo to Señor Ribeyro.

"Lima, April 12th, 1864.

"The undersigned, Special Commissary Extraordinary of Her Catholic Majesty, has had the honour to receive the note which his Excellency the Minister for Foreign Affairs of Peru has been pleased to address to him, under date of the 1st instant. In it the Government impugns the title of Special Commissary, on account of its not being in conformity with diplomatic rules and usages. The memorandum which the undersigned has addressed to the Representatives of the allied nations, and of which a copy is annexed, will explain to his Excellency the Minister for Foreign Affairs the significance that will be attached by Her Majesty's Government to the proceeding of that of the Republic under these critical circumstances.

"At one of the late sittings of the permanent Commission of the Congress, it was stated that the present Administration entertained the idea of contracting a loan of 70,000,000 dollars, which, from being so vastly beyond the requirements of the treasury, is, according to the opinions of influential politicians, for the purpose of obtaining means to oppose the just demands of Spain.

"The Peruvian Government will do what it thinks best, but the undersigned hopes that during his absence from Lima, the Queen's subjects will be treated with respect in the territory of the Republic, whatever may be the eventualities of the future. The moderation of the Government, of the authorities, and of the country in general, will give to that of Her Majesty the measure of the conduct which is to be followed hereafter ; and if, unfortunately, excesses shall be committed, the reprisals will be prompt, energetic, and decisive, for modern Spain is firmly resolved not to acquiesce in the ill-treatment of her sons, or in insult to her flag.

"The undersigned, &c.,

(*signed*) EUSEBIO DE SALAZAR Y MAZARREDO."

The "Special Commissary" would seem, after all, to think there was some force in the objection of the Peruvian Minister to his title, for in the remarkable production I have just quoted he adds to it the denomination of "Extraordinary," which does not certainly appear in the letter of his superior, who accredited him to

Peru. If by *extraordinary* he meant it to be understood that what he did and intended to do should be out of the *ordinary* course, he may have been right in assuming the cognomen, for it prepared people, as it were, to expect something eccentric and marvellous. The reader cannot fail also to remark the coolness with which this "extraordinary" individual reads a lecture on diplomacy to a foreign minister grown grey in the service of his country. The financial measures of the country are next brought under review, and because Peru is about to contract a loan for a larger amount than Señor Salazar in his wisdom deems necessary for the Republic, that sagacious personage arrives, with certain brother politicians, at the conclusion, that it is destined for a crusade against Spain. The impertinence of the concluding paragraph of his epistle, a mixture of inane pomposity and silly threats, would alone stamp the measure of the man. If language such as this had emanated from a person totally ignorant of Peru, it would have been a trifle more excusable, but Señor Salazar, who knew full well that his countrymen had always found protection and favour on Peruvian soil, lays himself open, by using it, to the greater censure, as he uttered calumnies well knowing at the time that they were nothing else. My readers, who have already perused the impartial communication of Mr. Jerningham, will have been enabled to form their own opinions of the manner in which Spaniards were treated in Peru, and for their further enlightenment I transcribe another letter from that gentleman, as fully worthy of praise as the former for its clearness, temperateness, and impartiality.

Mr. Jerningham to Earl Russell.

"Lima, April 28, 1864.

" My Lord,

" Since forwarding my despatch of the 13th instant by last mail, in which I transmitted to your Lordship copies of a correspondence which had taken place between the Peruvian Minister for Foreign Affairs and Señor Salazar y Mazarredo, who came here claiming to be received as a special and extraordinary Commissary from the Spanish Government to that of Peru, as well as of a memorandum addressed by Señor Mazarredo to the allied powers, I have received from the Peruvian Government through the official gazette, "El Peruano," copy of a note, herein inclosed, addressed by Señor Ribeyro to the Minister of State of Her Catholic Majesty, with reference to the proceedings of Señor Mazarredo and Admiral Pinzon since their advent to Peru.

" But I now regret to have to report that an event has occurred which has taken every one by surprise, viz., the forcible occupation of the Chincha Islands by the Spanish squadron under Admiral

Pinzon, in conjunction with M. Mazarredo, by which Peru is suddenly deprived of the chief source of her revenue.

"This occurrence has caused in Lima, the greatest possible irritation and dismay, as well as much trouble and astonishment amongst the foreign commercial body, especially the British members of it, who have much capital engaged in Peruvian trade, and who anticipate that much inconvenience and loss must ensue from this strange proceeding of the Spanish squadron.

"To give your Lordship exact information how this occupation was carried into effect, I beg to have the honour to forward copy of a letter received from Mr. John Dartnell, British Vice-Consul at Pisco, who happened to be at the time in the Chincha Islands.

"The day I received the copy of the memorandum (which I transmitted to your Lordship), M. Mazarredo left Lima, and I was told it was not known whither he had proceeded; but it now appears that he then repaired to Callao, went on board the Spanish war sloop "Covadonga," and feigning to sail for the north, proceeded afterwards in search of Admiral Pinzon's squadron, when he and the Admiral having met, they went to seize the Chincha Huano Islands (Chinchas). The Governor was then summoned to surrender, and menaced even with force, if he refused. He had not sufficient force to resist, and, therefore, was made prisoner; the Spanish flag was immediately substituted for the Peruvian ensign and hoisted in the islands, whilst the 150 Peruvians who had been left there to guard the wealth of the Republic, were, after a parley, allowed to depart to the mainland. The convicts were also dispatched to the coast, and the Peruvian sloop "Iquique," captured there by the Spaniards, was alone left with a complement of ten men to guard the spoils which had been so secretly and unceremoniously taken possession of by Admiral Pinzon and Commissary Salazar y Mazarredo.

"After the consummation of this act, the legality of which, no doubt, Her Majesty's Government and other civilized nations will discuss and decide upon, the Spanish squadron made their appearance off Callao in the morning of Saturday the 16th instant, when a note, without date, was despatched by Admiral Pinzon, accompanied by a declaration signed by him and M. Mazarredo of the 14th April, 1864, to Señor Ribeyro, the Peruvian Minister, copies of which are hereto annexed.

"On the same day Señor Ribeyro replied to the Admiral, copy herein inclosed, and his Excellency likewise addressed a circular to the Diplomatic Body, copy of which I also forward to your Lordship, together with my answer.

"I beg also to draw your Lordship's attention to the inclosure, giving the official correspondence between Admiral Pinzon and the Governor of the Chincha Islands, Señor Valle-Riestra.

"On the advent of the Spanish Admiral to Callao on the 16th inst., copies of this declaration were dispatched to the several members of the foreign Diplomatic Body residing in Lima.

"I was, however, first made acquainted with it that day by Capt. Douglas, of Her Majesty's ship "Shearwater," stationed at Callao, to whom M. Mazarredo had given a copy, which I have since learnt was intended for me.

"A few days ago the Members of the Diplomatic Body assembled at the house of the Dean, the United States Minister, Mr. Robinson, to take cognizance of the documents which had been forwarded to them individually, and after some consideration it was decided to issue a collective manifesto, copy of which 1 beg to inclose (and also of Señor Ribeyro's rejoinder), and as the members of the body signed it, I likewise came to the determination to append my name. This is, as stated in the paper, only ad interim, awaiting the instructions which our respective Governments may resolve on.

"The French Chargé d'Affaires for certain reasons did not sign the declaration of the Diplomatic Body, probably because M. Lesseps holds a double character here, being likewise charged with the protection of the Spanish subjects in Peru, and also because he may have imagined that in case he has hereafter to mediate, signing this paper might render his position less acceptable to the Spaniards.

"I also entertained the same idea; but as the United States Minister signed it, I did likewise. If I had refused, the British public in Peru, as well as the natives, would certainly have viewed my silence in a very objectionable light.

"The situation of Peru, owing to the event I have just mentioned, is of the gravest nature. At first there existed a strong feeling against the Government, and even a large assemblage of citizens thronged one evening the chief square of Lima, and crowded round the Palace, when the President, Pezet, was induced to appear at the window and address them.

"At Callao crowds appeared in the streets, and "Vivas" for "Castilla!" (meaning the former President of that name) were heard, and even an attempt at upsetting the Government was anticipated by people who argued that by mismanagement they had brought affairs to the present crisis.

"However, the Government have not been idle in endeavouring to instil confidence, and the Peruvians, friends, or oppositionists to the Government, feel the necessity in the present state of affairs of uniting together to resist what they consider a most serious aggression; for taking the Chincha Islands is, in fact, tantamount to seizing the chief wealth of Peru, for most of the treasures this land contains are still hidden in the mountains, or are to be sought for in the distant and thinly populated trans-Andine districts.

"If the Islands are to remain in the hands of the Spaniards, the detriment to trade and British capital circulating in Peru, reckoned at a rough estimate at nearly 100,000,000 dollars, will be most serious.

"The annual exportations of guano by the Peruvians is about from 16,000,000 to 18,000,000 dollars, and their expenditure about 23,000,000 dollars; consequently, unless they impose taxes and make loans, they remain with only 5,000,000 dollars to carry them through the financial year.

"The Spanish Declaration gives out that money contracts made hitherto with Peru by foreign companies will be respected; but what security have the British bondholders in this assertion, when Spain has not yet met her engagements with regard to part of her debt, and her paper, I am told, is not even admitted in the London Exchange.

"If the Islands are to be kept by Spain, this is a very serious affair for the Peruvians, but it is also a blow to British interests involved in Peruvian trade.

"What has likewise stung the Peruvian mind, especially in the seizure of the Chinchas, is the assertion contained in the Declaration, that the Spanish Admiral and Commissary have resolved to "revindicar" (retake or reconquer) the Islands, as if they still belonged to Spain, and were not, after the lapse of nearly forty years, an integral part of an independent State, which had been recognized as such by most of the civilized world.

"But what has been the reason assigned for the occupation of the Chinchas? Is it the attitude assumed by Peru with regard to Spain and her Agent?

"The Peruvian Government have apparently only declined to receive M. Mazarredo as Commissary, respecting which term they required explanations; but according to M. Ribeyro's note (inclosed in my last dispatch of the 13th instant), this Government consented willingly to receive him as a confidential Agent.

"Respecting the term " Commissary" I will not offer to undertake any remark; but, supposing the Peruvian Government has not found it advisable to receive M. Mazarredo in that character, surely some other might have been devised which could not have been objected to, and which might have prevented such an abrupt and regrettable termination of a mission, which reasonable persons might have supposed could have solved all difficulties and led to permanent friendship.

"The Memorandum sent home, contains a list of various grievances, &c., such as the ill-treatment of Spanish subjects; but even if all these turn out to be correct, surely the occupation of the Chinchas, which may be considered as impounding the Treasury of Peru, can hardly be considered in the light of a just material guarantee for enforcing redress.

"Unwilling to believe that the Spanish Government can entertain a permanent retention of the guano islands, I am led to look for a reason for this sudden and secret occupation, in the idea that the Spanish authorities may have effected it, as a means of pressure for causing Peru to give satisfaction for certain grievances.

"By this *coup de main*, Peru has been reduced for the moment to a helpless condition. Her squadron consists of one frigate and several steamers, but these, especially the frigate, are not in a state to resist or cope with the Spaniards, and although enthusiasm has been kindled to the highest pitch, they are unable to attack the Spanish squadron with any prospect of success. They have fortified Callao, in a sort of a way, and the war vessels they possess are placed under the protection of the Castle guns; besides, I am told they are going to plate some of their war steamers with iron rails, fashioned for the above purpose; but all this will take some time before it can be accomplished.

"The President has applied to the Congress for resources, and has been authorised to contract a loan of 50,000,000 dollars, and to raise the army to 30,000 men. A private loan has also been set on foot.

"The great Chilean capitalist Candamo has lent the Government 1,000,000 dollars, and the native commercial body is contributing towards it. General Castilla, who is in the south of Peru, has been sent for, probably to take the command of the army, and give his experienced counsel to Government.

"It is thought by some, although I have no reason to participate in the belief, that this affair has been concocted previously in the Spanish Peninsula; and if so, the tenacity of the Spaniards will probably cause them to keep their hold on the Chinchas until obliged to relinquish them by the friendly mediation of the great Powers, or till they are driven away by a sufficient force, which the Peruvians may eventually be able to collect in the course of time.

"The Spanish Admiral has retained as hostages the Governor and several officers of the Chinchas; but there appears no desire to injure or persecute the Spanish residents in Lima. They have even addressed a letter to that effect, and stating that retaining the above-mentioned officers as hostages is unnecessary.

"Since writing the above I hear that Admiral Pinzon has set at liberty all the Peruvians he took, and Señor Valle-Riestra, &c. are now in Lima.

"There has been a great show of patriotism, as far as offers of services go, both moral and physical: the Archbishop and Canons of the Cathedral and some of the clergy, the legal and other bodies, and numerous private citizens, have placed their services at the disposition of their country, so as to make use of them for the just rights of the Republic as may be deemed most fit.

"The Memorandum to which I have constantly alluded has now been printed in "El Peruano," and likewise Señor Ribeyro's answer to it, both of which I have the honour officially to forward to your Lordship.

"I have received from the French Chargé d'Affaires, M. de Lesseps, a copy, which I suppose is authentic (although not signed by any one to that effect), of Admiral Pinzon's answer to Señor Ribeyro's note of the 16th instant, which I now inclose to your Lordship.

"I have the honour also to inclose copy of a circular addressed to the Foreign Governments by Señor Ribeyro, dated the 26th instant, and published in the official Gazette "El Peruano" of this day, regarding the unfortunate incidents that have just taken place between the Peruvian Government and the Spanish authorities on this coast.
"I have, &c.
(*signed*)   WM. STAFFORD JERNINGHAM."

The despatch I have transcribed, joined to the other evidence adduced, amply prove that Señor Ribeyro did his best to maintain a friendly understanding with the impracticable man with whom he had to deal. Discovering at last that it was the vainest of hopes to conceive that the Spanish Commissary would listen to reason, he on the 13th of April addressed a despatch to the Minister of State of Her Catholic Majesty, to which, notwithstanding its length, I would beg my readers' careful attention. Its tone and style cannot but be considered calm and dignified, even when perused at this distance of time and far removed from the turmoil amid which it was indited; but it must be held as infinitely more praiseworthy, when we reflect that it was written at a period when the very existence of the Government was threatened, when mobs were parading the streets, and every class of Peruvian society, as described in Mr. Jerningham's letter, was shaken to its very centre.

From Señor Ribeyro, to the Minister of State of Her Catholic Majesty.

"Lima, April 13, 1864.

"EXCELLENT SIR,—Peru has long entertained a strong desire to re-establish her relations with Spain, a nation to which she is united by the bonds of affinity; but this often-expressed desire has been foiled by difficulties not easily to be set aside. The time has now come for the Government, as faithful interpreter of the wishes of the people whose destinies they govern, to address themselves directly to the Madrid Cabinet, in order to remove all the difficulties which have hitherto prevented the reconciliation of the two States so called upon by their origin and interests to live in perfect peace and harmony.

"The war was scarcely over in America, when independent nations were formed, which, in the exercise of their right, endeavoured by every means to attain to prosperity, and initiate themselves into the paths of industry and commerce. Peru made no exception to this enlightened policy. Her ports, fields, and cities, without any exception, were thrown open to all laborious foreigners; and Spaniards, although without any previous agreement, and as members of our Association, enjoyed and still enjoy the same freedom, respect and prerogatives as our own people. An enumeration of these facts, which are evident to all competent and impartial persons who have visited our country, might be made so as to prove them in a most victorious manner; but Her Catholic Majesty's Government, who so well know the proverbial mildness of the Peruvian character, the excellence of our laws and of our administrative organization, will no doubt not require such a work to be made, as it would not increase the useful knowledge possessed by them of all the regions of the continent.

"The benevolence of the Peruvian nation has been falsely interpreted by passionate functionaries and private persons, who, having found themselves deceived in their expectations, became gratuitous enemies of the country which had given them hospitality; but it was never believed that such statements would loosen the bonds which unite nations for their mutual good. In order to obviate and prevent fresh difficulties, which would perhaps relax existing ties and endanger peace, the undersigned, Minister for Foreign Affairs of Peru, has the honour to address the Spanish Minister of State, in order to give him some explanations, which, by their sincerity and frankness, cannot fail to induce the two Governments to come to an understanding, and to treat in a proper, frank, and harmonious manner.

"It has been observed, not without great sorrow, that for the last four years the Press of Spain publishes articles against Peru, which one person in the former country, in correspondence with another resident in this capital, is careful officiously to prepare. There is no imposture they do not assert, nor even which they do not transfigure, stating that the nation is without laws, customs, and morality, and that all the inhabitants are abandoned to the frenzy of a repugnant licentiousness, and that the Government is responsible for all these excesses. Lower in the scale than a barbarous nation, Peru is considered to be a den of bandits, where no right is respected, and where life is continually exposed. These calumnies, systematically spread abroad, may have produced a bad feeling in some persons, and have no doubt given rise to that dislike of the Peruvian authorities which has created difficulties to the prompt settlement of questions between the two countries.

"Let it be said, in passing, the motives for this conduct are to be found in ignoble passion, which is the more inveterate as it has no grounds whatsoever to justify it.

"When the Spanish squadron destined for the Pacific arrived at Callao, the Government extended that generous hospitality to it with which they receive their friends, and notwithstanding the alarm created by the motives attributed to that naval expedition, circumspection and common sense gained the victory over vague and malicious reports. Neither the most rigorous rules of etiquette, nor civilities of all sorts, nor a marked deference were omitted on the arrival of the sailors of the Peninsula, with whom the sons of Peru felt they had ties of blood which were formed in the most remote times. But this most refined politeness has not been properly met, nor the most insignificant demonstration made such as our society had a right to expect. The Admiral, chief of the squadron, to whom all, from the Government down to the private citizen, showed every sort of attention, used, from the first, a disdainful tone both with the authorities and private persons, and instead of studying our people and public men in order better to carry out the intentions of his Government, he avoided them, and accused them unjustly, surrounding himself by a special circle, which made his stay amongst us every day more intolerable. Anywhere else such acts would have led to fatal disagreements. Fortunately, notwithstanding this, the Peruvian Government were not wanting in the politeness necessary to dissipate fears and disturbances which would have retarded the good understanding between Peru and Spain.

"An unforeseen event, but a very ordinary one in every part of the world, however civilized, gave greater extension to the Admiral's already very extensive demands, and to those of the persons who were desirous of a conflict. A riot unfortunately broke out at a farm called Talambo, situated in the north, between some Spanish colonists and the natives, in which a Spaniard and a Peruvian were killed, and some others wounded.

"As soon as the Supreme Administration heard of the event, they cast aside their important occupations, and ordered their delegates to do their duty by apprehending the culprits, and investigating the matter in order to punish the guilty. They were not compelled to do this, but were stimulated by a desire to see justice properly executed.

"The matter has been set on foot, and although not quite terminated, measures are being taken to clear up the facts, and demonstrate clearly who are the real authors of the crime.

"So far there has been no denial of justice nor culpable delay, the only cases which, according to international right, authorize diplomatic reclamations. The affair of Talambo has, however, been painted in such colours that, to judge by these narrations, Peru would be the last of nations. But, fortunately, unquestionable testimony and documents prove sufficiently that our criminal statistics bear no proportion to our population, and that fewer crimes are committed in the nation thus harshly treated than in others more advanced in civilization.

"The enemies of the country—for those that give absurd information must be considered as such—availed themselves of the Talambo affair; and M. Pinzon, lending an ear to passionate assertions, has, it is affirmed, stated to Her Catholic Majesty's Government that it is a most hideous event, that the authorities have not moved in the matter, and pointed out the risks which are always run by Spanish subjects. It is not strange that persons ignorant of our institutions, or badly affected towards the Government, should judge in this manner; but it is strange, and in no slight degree, that an authorized Chief, charged with a civilizing and friendly mission, should disappoint, or tend to disappoint good feelings engendered on both sides.

"The Talambo affair has been the cause of continual censure, as has also the circumspect conduct of the Tribunals, not excepting the Supreme Court of Justice, so worthy of veneration for its wisdom, prestige, and traditional purity. The Spanish Consul, to whom this Department communicated the state of the case, although he has no diplomatic character, and it was only done out of deference and to preserve good harmony between the two nations, allowed himself, in a note dated the 25th of February last, to make offensive allusions to a body which is the safeguard of all right, the deposit of all judicial science, and which enjoys the confidence of both the Government and the people. He also made a protest, which being only a matter of pure form, did not affect the case. This happened just as the sentences of the first tribunal of the Republic were being hailed with public applause, owing to their impartiality and justice.

"It is necessary to dwell a little over these points, not with a view of provoking replies and engendering fresh differences, which this Cabinet wishes to terminate irrevocably, but in order to call attention to certain incidents which throw more than sufficient light to bear witness to the uprightness and loyalty with which Peru always deals with the other nations of the earth.

"Nor is it to be expected that in this country, where so many Spaniards and foreigners of all classes and conditions live quietly and easily at work without let or hindrance, many possessed of the blessings of fortune, that these should be exposed to frequent danger, as some have wished to make out, or should continually run risks from ill-nature. If it were so there would be neither that spontaneous emigration which flows to our country, nor would those large capitals be amassed which we find in the hands of those who are not Peruvians, nor those frank acknowledgments of content be made, by which more than once strangers have testified to the honour of justice;—acknowledgments which have fully vindicated the honour of the Republic, which is wounded with so little consideration. We have a proof of this in the speech made by a distinguished Spaniard on board the frigate "Resolucion," when, in the name and presence of a great number of his fellow-countrymen, he congratulated Admiral Pinzon on his fortunate arrival in these waters.

"The Government of Peru, as well as all the society, was very far from admitting that a common act of naturalization should serve as a pretext for inventing absurd stories against a country which prides itself, amongst other things, on its character for hospitality. The Peruvian people greet all their guests with marks of candour, and offer to all their riches, without reserve; but they naturally show themselves more demonstrative with Spaniards, whom they look on as members of their own family, and whom they distinguish by especial marks of preference, as well in their domestic and social dealings as in the laws themselves, which give them concessions with open-handed liberality. So far from enmity to Spain and her sons, being exhibited here, so far even from mere quiet intercourse, our people display towards them great tolerance, much affection and vast generosity.

"When Señor Salazar appeared in this capital, various and contradictory accounts were given of his mission, but the Cabinet waited for his official presentation to judge with certainty, and proceeded with the circumspection which they are accustomed to use towards the Representatives of friendly nations, since such they consider Spain, in spite of its not having been defined at all explicitly in what position the two nations are placed on account of events which we will not now speak of.

"As Peru never has wished for, nor wishes for, anything more sincerely than a good understanding with that nation which formerly was her mother-country, she hoped, not without sufficient reason, that the mission of Señor Mazarredo, in spite of its special character, might clear a path for a formal, definitive and explicit reconciliation. The Government, far from raising obstacles that might retard the conclusion of this important result, was disposed to offer every facility for coming to an understanding with the Envoy; and when the latter presented himself in order to deliver his credentials to the Undersigned, he assured him that his intentions were disinterested and noble, and that he was nothing more than the faithful organ of the views of the country and the administration. This act of marked courtesy, as well as others even more significant, was, indeed, not returned in the same manner, because Señor Mazarredo turned his attention to the consideration of certain questions and certain persons in the country, which, had they continued, might perhaps have led us to a fatal result. The Undersigned accepted the explanation which this gentleman made upon the matter, when he called his attention to it, and begged him to avoid discussions which might be left for another opportunity. Thus ended the only interview with Señor Mazarredo.

"His credentials, contained in the dispatch of his Excellency the President of the Council and Principal Secretary of State of Her Catholic Majesty, were read without passion and without any ulterior view; but the Cabinet, without ceasing to accept Señor Mazarredo in that character, made an observation which, rightly interpreted, would have left the parties completely satisfied. It told him, with the greatest moderation, that his mission being purely confidential, they would receive him as a confidential agent of Spain, because, in the course of negociations, the title of Commissary might offer embarrassments which, in the common interest, it was necessary to avoid at any cost. It was not proposed that he should change the title, because this was not in his power, but in that of his Government, but then he should receive the explanation that was made to him to be considered, even without attention to the name given to his mission, only as a confidential agent: this step was necessary, because before this Señor Tavira had come accredited in this character, in order to satisfy a desire generally expressed, and because in reality, the title of Commissary was not the most fit to enter upon certain superior negotiations of this nature. If the answer had been that the question was of little moment, since, under one name or another, the aim of the Spanish Government was to come to an understanding by the means of a confidential agent, every thing would have become smooth, and affairs would haply have taken a different course. That your Excellency may perceive the sincerity of the Peruvian Government, a copy of the note addressed to Señor Mazarredo is enclosed, in which there is not a single phrase which is not decorous and worthy, and in which the purest cordiality is revealed.

"Nevertheless, Señor Salazar y Mazarredo addressed to the undersigned a note dated yesterday, accompanied by a memorandum which he affirms he has sent to the allied nations, in which he recapitulates a number of events and considerations, political as well as historical, to prove the constant enmity which the Governments of Peru, during the forty years of its independence, has manifested against Spain. As both of these documents were sent to this office late in the day, and under the circumstance of Señor Mazarredo having left this capital and embarked at Callao on board the "Covadonga," it was not possible to answer them properly, especially the second, because the shortness of the time, as the mail starts for Europe to day, does not allow of a discussion, which could not but be conclusive for Peru, which has from every point of view justice on her side. The undersigned will not omit, however, to make some reflections to show that Señor Mazarredo, taking for truth simple conjectures and isolated sayings utterly destitute of anything like truth, by lavishing abuse upon the nation and its authorities, which they certainly do not deserve, betrays the prejudiced mind of a diplomatist to whom has been attributed for some time the publication of certain articles in the Madrid newspapers, highly offensive to the dignity of a country whose culture has fortunately not been surpassed. The Government of Peru, neither to resist the demands of the Government of the Peninsula, nor for any other purpose, has had the idea of raising a loan of 70,000,000 dollars. The same Deputy who presented a motion on this account to the Legislative Commission withdrew it immediately, convinced of the inexactness and falseness of the rumour which had been maliciously spread. The negociation of a loan for so large an amount as that referred to, is of such a nature that it cannot be effected silently or clandestinely. Whatever might have been the precautions adopted to keep it secret, it must necessarily reveal itself, and become public property.

"Señor Mazarredo's assertion has not the support of a single fact, nor even of the slightest indication to show that the Government had entertained such an idea. Time will prove the falseness of a proposition which Señor Mazarredo should have examined previously in order not to fall into a mistake which compromises his prudence and outrages a Government, which up to this time has not given reason to raise a doubt as to its loyalty.

"Peru and its present Government had so much confidence in the moderation of those persons who direct Spanish policy, that it did not think even for a moment that affairs would have arrived at the lamentable state in which they now are. In spite of the course which they have taken, there are some people who comfort themselves in thinking that the fortunate occurrences which have lately taken place since the arrival of Señor Mazarredo will be carefully studied by the Spanish Government, who, no doubt, will see in all the steps and wise measures of which the undersigned has made use, the signs of good feeling in accordance with the national dignity, rather than acts of enmity against the Spaniards.

"Señor Mazarredo, on leaving Lima, has left in his note a cause of deep grief for the Government of Peru, attributing to it evil dispositions in entering into an arrangement with the Government of your Excellency; and this regret becomes the greater as there are certain allusions relative to the insecurity of Spanish subjects resident in the Republic. They shall continue, as up to the present, protected by the laws; they shall always be the object of a cordial and sincere hospitality; they shall not be injured either in person or property; and they shall be left in the exercise of their industry, and in the enjoyment of the many benefits of a country happy in its climate, and happy in the conditions of its enlightened policy.

"And these guarantees, granted without restriction of any sort, are not the result of the terror which Señor Mazarredo attempted to inspire, by making reprisals which shall never take effect, since Peru will act in a sense of justice, and since Spain is not able to cease paying, as she always has done, a homage to virtue, to reason, and to right.

"The undersigned reserves to himself the reasons and arguments of greater consideration until he shall reply to the memorandum, which he will do, so soon as the affairs of the moment allow him; and he concludes the present communication in the hope that its contents may be a further proof of his just and upright conduct. If, unfortunately (which he cannot bring himself to believe), this frank exposition is not attended to, Peru puts her faith in the justice of her cause, in the incontestable testimony of real facts themselves, and the generous sentiments and opinions of civilized and impartial people.

"With the sentiments, &c.
(*signed*)   " JUAN ANTONIO RIBEYRO."

The course of events leads naturally to the conclusion, that if the seizure of the Chinchas was not a step previously arranged in the Peninsula, it was resolved upon by the Special Commissary in order to make further friendly negociations impossible. The unseemly haste which he used, may perhaps be attributed to his apprehension that the voice of reason and common sense would make itself heard by the Spanish Cabinet.

It is a subject of regret to very many persons that Admiral Pinzon should have been made a party to the taking of the Islands. All who know him cannot but believe he must have acted in the matter under a misapprehension, for his brave and generous nature, to which Mr. Jerningham in his letter to Earl Russell of the 13th May bears witness, would have scorned to attack a defenceless place, without positive orders also from his Queen, unless the whole affair had been grossly misrepresented. It is therefore reasonable to suppose that when Señor Salazar wrote to him at Valparaiso, he must have exaggerated both the authority with which he was invested, and the conduct of the Peruvians with respect to him.

The Memorandum of the Special Commissary has been so often alluded to, and it is indeed not only in a diplomatic point of view, but in that of plain, common sense, so unique a production to emanate from a Government Envoy, that, but for its great length, I would have produced it in its entirety. As, however, my space will not allow of such a step, I will transcribe literally those portions to which my comments will be directed. Before doing so, I may observe, that Señor Salazar y Mazarredo never made known the precise object of his visit to Peru. As the foregoing letter has explained, he had but one interview with the Peruvian Minister for Foreign Affairs, during which, precisely as in his writings, instead of argument he used invective, and had to be reminded that the uttering tirades against private individuals was not precisely the mode to open diplomatic negociations. His truthfulness and temper may also be estimated from the fact that he had no hesitation, when a point was raised as to the meaning to be attached to his title of "Special Commissary" to call the settlement of this necessary question, *a refusal to receive him*. The very course taken by his vessel on quitting the roads of Callao was a deception,—for having, while in sight of the townspeople, steered in one direction, he is afterwards found in a completely opposite one; and the close of his "mission of peace," is distinguished by a proceeding which common-minded people style an act of piracy, but which goes forth to the world under the grand but unfortunate term of a " revindication."

Señor Salazar's Memorandum was ably answered by Señor Ribeyro on the 20th of April, but as that gentleman has mainly contented himself with refuting the calumnies cast upon the Peruvian *Government*, I will direct my remarks to the misrepresentation of facts in the affair of Talambo. I have already, on a former occasion, alluded to this occurrence, but I will now examine it a little more in detail.

And first of all, I cannot help remarking that, taking their cue from each other, Spaniards persist in depicting this Talambo riot under false colours. They repeat the same story, with the usual additions and exaggerations, but clearly show that they have not taken the trouble to examine and judge for themselves. As I fortunately have the whole of the debates, to which it gave rise, before me, and have given them the most patient investigation, I am enabled to speak upon the subject with a certain degree of confidence.

The Memorandum says—I quote the exact words:—" That on the 4th of August, eighteen (Basques) being at the house of the proprietor (Señor Salcedo) who had called them in to settle their differences, on a sudden some seventy armed men entered into the Court and rushed upon the defenceless Spaniards. One of them, Ormazabal, fell dead; and four others were wounded—two so seriously that they received extreme unction. The house of the dead man was pillaged, and one woman, the wife of Eguren, and her son, died in a few days. After this butchery was completed, they placed the villains as sentinels to keep close watch over the colonists, continuing to treat them inhumanly."

2. " That it is a public and notorious fact that Don Manuel Salcedo observed the murderers from the balcony of his house; that his steward, Carmen Valdez, was the man who headed the band; that he distributed to them the rewards of this treachery by order of his master, and that for many days they were lodged and maintained at the cost of Salcedo."

3. " That the Basques, wounded and others, remained for 17 days, viz.: from the 4th to the 21st of August, guarded by these same murderers."

4. " That a quarter of an hour before the catastrophe, the Governor of *Chepen*, the chief place of the district, breakfasted with Don Manuél Salcedo, and that on leaving the estate he met the murderers without putting any obstacle in the way of their plans."

5. " That Manuel Suarez, the Juez de Aguas of the estate, and two servants of the Governor of Chepen, were among the murderers."

6. " That when the Justice of the Peace of Chepen went to the estate to investigate (or take evidence) he remained four days without taking any proceedings."

7. " That when the Justice afterwards received the declarations of the wounded colonists and their companions they were still in the custody of the armed assassins."

8. " That the turn given to the affair at Talambo in the Supreme Court of Justice has a tendency to put off indefinitely the punish-

ment of the criminals, and has given rise to an energetic protest from the Spanish Consul in Lima."

The eight charges here transcribed form the pith of the accusations contained in the Memorandum respecting the riot at Talambo, the main cause of the present hostile attitude of Spain.

The evidence is at variance with nearly *all* Señor Mazarredo's so-called facts, which, from mere hearsay, and coloured to suit his own purpose, he has, with singular effrontery, set forth in a document addressed to Foreign Powers as a justification for an act of spoliation.

To begin, it is simply untrue that the 18 Basques who met on the 4th of August at Señor Salcedo's house, had been summoned there by him; it is also untrue that when there, they were attacked by 70 armed men. The evidence shows that the Spaniards were met together at the "Hacienda" at the request of Miner (a Basque), who, a few hours previously, had assaulted Señor Salcedo himself, and, being turned out by that gentleman, was trying to organize a conspiracy of his countrymen to take Señor Salcedo's life. A proof of this is to be found in the fact that *they were armed*, and not, as the "Special Commissary" asserts, "*defenceless*;" and that they used their arms is equally evident, for on the approach of the Peruvians (labourers, be it observed, like themselves), Fano (a Basque) fired upon them and shot Rosario Salazar, one of the foremost, who instantly fell dead.

What degree of credit then can be attached to the assertions of a man, who will unscrupulously affirm that the Peruvians in this case were the aggressors, when the first shot was fired by the Spaniards, and the first victim to fall was a Peruvian? Why did not the Commissary of Queen Isabella II. state this most important circumstance? Or did he in his wisdom think his case would be all the better for its suppression?

It is again untrue that the wounded Spaniards received extreme unction. Their hurts were not of a nature to require the performance of so serious a ceremony; but more than that, *there was not a Catholic priest within miles of the locality!*

The plundering of Ormazabal's house (the Spaniard shot in the fray) has been proved to be simply false; but the death of the wife and son of Eguren is a statement almost ludicrous, in its employment of a fact with a view to draw from it false inferences. The poor woman, it appears, *died in childbirth ;* her labour, perhaps, hastened by the excitement occasioned by the disturbances. Admitting, for the sake of argument, that it was so, is this a charge to be brought against a Government, and to form with others of a like trivial nature a *casus belli?* Surely, after this, we may cease to regard the voyage to Lilliput as a creation of the brain; we may safely adopt it as history, and think, that the dispute about breaking an egg at the large or the small end was a legitimate cause for war!

With respect to the labourers of Señor Salcedo keeping guard over the Basques implicated in the riot, it is undoubtedly true; but their surveillance only extended to a period of *four* and not *seventeen* days, and the measure was rightly deemed a proper one in the absence of a regular police, both in order to prevent fresh disturbances and the escape of the guilty parties.

From the evidence it does not appear that Don Manuel Salcedo was a witness to this unhappy disturbance.

The evidence does not show that rewards were distributed to the rioters by order of Señor Salcedo.

The assertion of Señor Salazar y Mazarredo that the Governor of Chepen breakfasted with Señor Salcedo on the morning in question, and that on leaving the "Hacienda" he met the assassins without attempting to frustrate their diabolical plans, rests upon the Special Commissary's word alone. None of the witnesses examined hinted at such a matter; and the circumstance is so improbable that it may well be left to the judgment of the impartial.

It is true that the Juez de Aguas and two of the servants of the Governor were engaged in the affray; but as we have already shown that the party of Peruvians were fired upon when proceeding to arrest the riotous Basques, the insinuation of Señor Salazar only reacts upon himself and the cause he attempts to uphold, inasmuch as it proves that not even the presence of constituted authorities was sufficient to restrain the Spaniards.

Before quitting this ungrateful subject, I cannot refrain from mentioning in reply to Señor Salazar's assertions as to the general ill-treatment of the "peaceful" Spanish labourers engaged by Señor Salcedo, and who, as I have elsewhere described, so unscrupulously broke their contract, that many of these men who landed upon Peruvian shores penniless and shoeless, are at this present time on the road to, if not actually in the possession of a decent competency. Some of them are reputed possessors of capital ranging from 2000 to 8000 dollars, and Sorazu, who was one of the ringleaders of the riot, is in the enjoyment of a revenue of 600 dollars per annum, paid him by the "Beneficencia," for his services as steward of a hospital!

The seizure of the Chincha Islands,* without the slightest previous notice, has, it may well be imagined, caused serious injury to the Peruvian Government, who, by the loss of four-fifths of their revenue, are likely to fail in their engagements, through this wanton act of spoliation. The mischief, however, does not stop there. The loss to many foreign merchants will be equally severe; and it is no wonder that the event should excite amongst them the very strongest feelings.

On the 16th of May a meeting was called, and was presided over by Mr. William de Courcy. Among the gentlemen present

---

* Some information respecting the value of these Islands will be found in the Appendix.

I may mention Messrs. Higginson, Lewis, Seymour, O'Connor, and seventy others, doing business in Peru. At this assembly not only was warm sympathy expressed for the Peruvian Government, but means were likewise devised to meet the difficulty by force.

The Diplomatic Body residing in Lima, animated by the same spirit, made a declaration on the 20th of April, which runs as follows:—

"The undersigned Foreign Ministers who compose the Diplomatic Body in Lima, being met together under the presidency of their eldest member, the Honourable Mr. Robinson, Envoy Extraordinary and Minister Plenipotentiary for the United States;

"Having taken into their serious consideration the declaration issued on the 14th instant, in the anchorage of the Chincha Islands by the Commissary of Her Catholic Majesty, and the Commander-in-Chief of the squadron in the Pacific; and bearing in mind,—

"That the Resolutions contained in that document were come to without previous declaration of war, ultimatum, or other formalities which are dictated by the public right of nations;

"That one of the reasons adduced for the occupation is the right which the Commissary and General in command attribute to their nation, to recover the islands belonging to Peru;

"The undersigned, in the impossibility of receiving instructions from their respective Governments in so short a time,

" Declare,—

" 1st. That they deplore sincerely that the Commissary and Commander-in-Chief should not have regulated their proceedings by the rules prescribed by international law in such cases.

"2nd. That they do not admit the right of recovery which has been invoked as one of the reasons for the occupation, but will continue to consider the Chincha Islands as belonging to the Peruvian Government until their respective Governments shall decide what they consider right.

" Signed at Lima on the 20th April, 1864.

(*signed*) " CHRISTOPHER ROBINSON, Envoy Extraordinary and Minister Plenipotentiary of the United States to Peru.

"J. DE LA CRUZ BENEVENTI, Minister Plenipotentiary of Bolivia to Peru, and named in the same character for the American Congress.

" THOS. R. ELDRIDGE, Chargé d'Affaires and Consul-General of His Majesty the King of Hawaii to Peru.

"WM. STAFFORD JERNINGHAM, Her Britannic Majesty's Chargé d'Affaires and Consul-General to Peru.

" J. NICOLAS HURTADO, Chargé d'Affaires of Chili to Peru."

The foregoing declaration was received at Lima with the warmest demonstrations of delight and approval. The President, through Señor Ribeyro, expressed the gratitude of the nation in these terms:—

"Lima, April 21, 1864.

"The undersigned, Minister for Foreign Affairs of Peru, had the honour to receive from the hands of the Chargés d'Affaires of His Majesty the King of Hawaii and of Chili, the declaration which they were pleased to present to him in the names of their Excellencies the foreign Diplomatic Body residing in Lima, in which, after taking into serious consideration the declaration which was sent on the 14th instant from the anchorage of the Chincha Islands by the Commissary of Her Catholic Majesty and the Commander-in-Chief of the Spanish squadron in the Pacific, the said excellent and honourable Ministers have thought proper to declare in a solemn manner—

"1. That they lament sincerely that the Commissary and the Commander-in-Chief have not proceeded in accordance with what is prescribed by international law for such cases; and,

"That they do not accept the right of revindication which has been appealed to as one of the foundations of the occupation; but that they shall continue to look upon the Chincha Islands as belonging to the Peruvian Republic, until their respective Governments shall determine what they shall consider expedient.

"The Government of Peru, in protesting against the acts of violence committed in the Republic by foreign naval forces, was convinced that its procedure was founded on those just claims which depend on imprescriptible and sacred rights. It was its duty to maintain those rights, and if it be considered that they are bound up with those of the independence and sovereignty of Peru, the most excellent gentlemen to whom the undersigned has the honour to address himself, will readily feel how satisfactory it has been to his Government to see those rights recognized and solemnly supported by the enlightened and most competent opinion of the Diplomatic Body resident in Lima.

"The Peruvian Government, with such a favourable precedent, cannot but feel its faith and confidence increased in the issue of the great question which has brought out the above-mentioned declaration, and also feels itself strengthened on finding this honourable body on its side, in the maintenance of those saving forms which have been trampled upon by the Spanish Commander and Commissioner, and are prescribed by the law of nations as the ultimate guarantee of international intercourse.

"The undersigned has very great pleasure in fulfilling the grateful duty of making known those feelings which his Government cherishes; and by order of his Excellency the President of the Republic, who highly estimates all that is favourable to the interests of the Republic in yesterday's declaration, he inserts them in this note, in order that those thanks may be public and manifest, which he has directed him to communicate to the Diplomatic Body, for the noble and spontaneous manner in which this declaration was made.

"The undersigned requests his Excellency the Envoy Extraordinary and Minister Plenipotentiary of the United States, the Dean of the Diplomatic Body, to accept for himself this manifestation of the gratitude of the Peruvian Government, and to communicate the same to the representatives of the friendly nations who signed the declaration with him.

(*signed*) "JUAN ANTONIO RIBEYRO."

Nothing of particular moment transpired from the date of the protest of the Diplomatic Body, until the 7th of May, when the British sloop "Shearwater" arrived at the Chincha Islands, having on board the Ministers of France, England, and Chili. Those gentlemen had come to the Islands with a view to effect, if possible, a settlement of the existing difficulties. Admiral Pinzon at first received them with a little coolness, being under the impression that the Peruvian Government had sent them to intercede; but on the assurance of M. de Lesseps that they had come spontaneously, he changed his tone and entered into negociations. As a proof of good feeling he gave up to them the "Iquique," captured on the 14th of April, in order that it might be restored to the Peruvians. The Spanish officials at the same time, by way of explanation of such a proceeding, issued the following Memorandum:—

"The events which took place on the Chincha Islands on the 14th April have been properly explained in the documents which are before the Republic.

"The Representatives of the Queen have always trusted that the moderation of the Peruvian people, acknowledged in the memorandum of the 12th of that month, together with the natural calmness of their minds, will ultimately put the question on its true footing.

"To-day that the Diplomatic Corps residing in Lima has been pleased to depute to the Chincha Islands a Committee of its body, composed of the Ministers of Great Britain, France, and Chili, to confer upon the present situation, the undersigned declare again of their own accord, that Spain has no pretensions to interfere with the form of the Peruvian Government, and that the occupation of the Islands by way of reprisals, until her Majesty's Government should decide, was, for especial reasons, preferable to other acts of hostility, which, by causing bloodshed, would render the settlement of the pending questions difficult.

"The Representatives of the Queen have not in the smallest degree prevented the traders of the Republic and of the Peruvian dependencies from attending to their transactions, and discharging their duties, as if the question were one of interest appertaining to friendly nations; and from the first day they have decidedly forbidden the loading of any guano on boats which have not the visa of the Callao authorities, who also, in accordance with the existing instructions, legalize all the documents of the captains previously to their departure for the places they are bound to.

"Being desirous to furnish a proof of their good wishes, the undersigned request the Ministers of England, France, and Chili, to be pleased likewise to make known to their colleagues—

"That the "Iquique" has been restored;

"That the Spanish squadron will keep on the defensive, if it be not compelled to do otherwise, and that a term of forty-eight hours will be given to the respective authorities, if there shall be any necessity to bring hostilities against any part of the Republic.

"That Her Majesty's Government, as it was verbally stated on the 16th of April to the chiefs of the foreign naval stations, will not claim the payment of any debt of private persons which does not possess the following conditions, namely, Spanish origin and continuity and present existence of rights in Spanish subjects;

"That the debts or claims of private persons which in any way admit of doubts, shall be laid before a Mixed Commission;

"And, lastly, that the reports which represent Spain to be desirous of establishing European dynasties in Peru, or in any other of the non-recognised Republics in America, are destitute of any sort of foundation.

"Anchorage of the Chincha Islands, on board the frigate 'Resolucion,' May 7, 1864.
 (*signed*) " LUIS H. PINZON.
   EUSEBIO DE SALAZAR Y MAZARREDO."

Señor Ribeyro refused to receive back the little sloop " Iquique," unless the Islands were likewise restored, and judging from the subjoined letter of Mr. Jerningham to Earl Russell, the only result obtained by, or likely to accrue from, the action of the Diplomatic Body, was to receive from the parties in dispute the customary polite thanks for their interference.

Mr. Jerningham to Earl Russell.

"Lima, May 13, 1864.

" MY LORD,

"Upon our return to Lima from the Chincha Islands, the Dean of the Diplomatic Corps, Mr. Robinson, with two of its members, waited on his Excellency, Señor Ribeyro, at his private residence, to inform him that the Peruvian war-sloop " Iquique" had been made over by Admiral Pinzon to the Diplomatic Body, and had been brought to Callao, and that they consequently presented to the Peruvian Government the vessel that had been restored.

"In this interview Admiral Ribeyro seems to have been rather short, and refused on the spot to receive the " Iquique."

" She is at present in Callao, but I believe that it is determined by the Diplomatic Body to return her now to Admiral Pinzon, which step will require a great deal of tact, as he may conceive the non-acceptance as an offence offered to himself, and perhaps to the Diplomatic Body, and might, therefore, consider himself released from his declaration of remaining at present on the defensive.

"It is a great pity that when Admiral Pinzon has, by the act of restoring the "Iquique," although without saluting the Peruvian flag, made a sort of step towards an arrangement, that this Government has not received the vessel under protest, and thus not permitted a fresh difficulty to be added to the many others in the road to reconciliation.

"The pressure from without has been the reason, and they fear a revolution if they do anything which they apprehend may possibly be disapproved of by the public mind, which at present is in a most excited state.

"I have, &c.,
(*signed*) "WM. STAFFORD JERNINGHAM."

On the very day of the signature of the joint Memorandum which accompanied the restoration of the "Iquique," viz., on the 7th of May, Señor Salazar y Mazarredo announced his resignation of the post of "Special Commissary," by means of the following note appended to the document alluded to:—

"Señor Salazar y Mazarredo, Commissary of Her Catholic Majesty in Peru, and her Minister in Bolivia, wishes it to be publicly known that he has made the sacrifice of his *amour propre* to the importance of the questions in debate between Spain and Peru, having resigned by the last post the appointments which he owed to the confidence of the Queen, because he is of opinion that when serious conflicts take place, men who respect themselves ought, in the nineteenth century, to place their Governments in a position to conquer without embarrassment, and with a lofty spirit of impartiality, all the difficulties which may offer themselves, always unmindful of persons and dwelling only on principles."

On the following day, Señor Salazar quitted the "Resolucion" and embarked on board the "Shearwater" for Callao. He reached that place on the 9th, and shifted his quarters to the "Leander," on board of which vessel he remained till the 13th of May, when he began that eventful, nay miraculous journey, the narrative of which it is now my purpose to examine.

PART SECOND.

THE VOYAGE HOME.—PERSONAL ADVENTURES.

The circular of Señor Don J. F. Pacheco to the Representatives of Her Catholic Majesty at Foreign Courts, dated Madrid, the 24th of June, 1864, was, as I have elsewhere mentioned, accompanied by a despatch of Señor Salazar y Mazarredo, giving an account of his voyage home, and the perils he encountered in the course of it. This is so singular a revelation that I propose to examine it in detail, applying, as I go on, my personal knowledge of the events and scenes he describes by way of testing their accuracy.

His narrative commences thus:—

"On the 8th of May I arrived at Callao with Señor Lora, a midshipman (the bearer of despatches for the Island of Cuba), on board her Britannic Majesty's corvette "Shearwater," commanded by Mr. Gordon Douglas, in company of the Ministers of France, Great Britain, and Chili, who had made a voyage to the Chincha Islands for the purpose of a conference with General Pinzon and myself. On the 9th I shifted my quarters to the British war frigate "Leander," from whose Commander, Commodore Harvey, I received,—as I had already received from Mr. Douglas,—the politest attentions. I remained on board the latter vessel till the 13th—the day for the starting of the Panama steamer, by which I intended returning to Spain.

"On the 12th, I received private advices to the effect that I must be cautious, as something was hatching against my person; and the Chancelier of the French Legation, Mr. Vion, confirmed this intelligence, advising me among other things that I ought not to go on board the packet at the spot, (near the Mole) where she lay at anchor, and counselling me to beg the Captain to take me from on board the "Leander" itself."

If the lines just quoted are intended by Señor Salazar to substantiate the charge which the Spanish Minister asserts, "*eclipses all the other charges which Spain conceives that she has against Peru*," I feel satisfied that all serious men will agree with me that the vague suspicions thus set forth are not only insufficient to support a grave accusation, but they strengthen the doubt as to the goodness of the other causes which have led Spain to her present hostile attitude towards Peru. It is not perhaps surprising that a man like Salazar, who, during the time that the events to which he alludes were taking place, was labouring under a degree of nervous excitement bordering on distraction, should exaggerate the position and see danger and menace where they did not exist, but it is astonishing that a Minister, in the calm retreat of his own cabinet, should be found ready to endorse the accusations against Peru, although founded upon the merest hearsay and conjecture.

Admitting, for the sake of argument, that Señor Salazar was justified in believing that a plot was hatching against his person, still it must be held as most strange that private individuals should have been in possession of the secret days, nay weeks, before it was to be realized; and if such a plot were contemplated, what right had he to infer that the Government of Peru was a party to it? For he does not allege that the parties who were so anxious for his safety, informed him *where* the plot was hatching, or *who* were the parties aiding or abetting it.

The only ground upon which Señor Salazar can base his charge against the Peruvian authorities must be sought for in his own notions of self-importance, which will not permit him to believe that a private individual would dare to conspire against his life. Although a little reflection might have taught him, that national insults such as those which he had heaped upon the Peruvian flag, had more than once met with condign punishment at the hands of obscure enthusiasts, without endeavouring to instil into Señor Pacheco's mind the idea that the "plot" was set on foot by the Government of Peru, and thus create a greater cause of complaint against the Republic than any that had hitherto been alleged against her.

The narrative thus proceeds:—

"On the morning of the 13th, the English merchant ship "Dauntless" cast anchor in the Bay, having on board Señor Cerruti, Professor of Languages to the midshipmen of the frigate "Resolucion," who, on the advice of General Pinzon, was to accompany me to Europe in the capacity of private Secretary. As soon as his arrival became known, the authorities at Callao endeavoured to get him into their power; but the Commodore, who had notice of the outrage contemplated upon the British flag, sent an officer on to prevent it, who arrived so opportunely, that he almost snatched him from the hands of the Peruvian soldiers."

This part of Señor Salazar's letter is a mixture of truth and misrepresentation. When Lieutenant Henry McInroy came on board the "Dauntless," he was courteously received by Señor José Leon, the Deputy-Captain of the Port, who, on being informed that Señor Cerruti had sent to the frigate "Leander" for a boat to take him off, said at once, "Well, he may go; but I protest." Before leaving, the English Lieutenant, the Deputy, and Señor Cerruti had a parting glass, which they drank to the toast of "A speedy settlement to the existing difficulties."

No "snatching" occurred, nor was there occasion for it. It is true, that prior to the *arrival* of the authorities, certain parties on board undertook to kidnap the private Secretary, but with what justice or right can the Government of Peru be blamed for the acts of private individuals? Moreover, even if Señor Salazar's statement were the exact truth, I doubt the right of the Spanish Cabinet to interfere in the matter, for the private Secretary is not a Spaniard, nor did he travel with a Spanish passport, and as the whole affair occurred on board of an English vessel, it would be the province of the Government of Great Britain, and not that of Spain, to interfere in the matter.

And here I cannot refrain from inquiring how it is that Señor Salazar, who is so lavish in his praise of those who assisted him either by word or deed, has no commendation left for Mr. William Corwan, the Master of the "Dauntless," who broke the standing rules of the Port of Callao for the purpose of befriending the private Secretary of the Spanish Commissary, thus enabling that gentleman to save the despatches which the Commissary asserts were judged by the Peruvian Government of so high a value that they were willing to give 22,000 dollars to emissaries in order to induce them to steal the "coveted documents?" And wherefore is it, that Señor Salazar omits to mention that Captain Corwan, on being offered the sum of 100 dollars for his trouble, flatly refused it, and with a dignity well becoming a noble sailor, asserted that gratitude and not gold was the motive which had induced him to act as he had done towards Señor Cerruti? And again, why does Señor Salazar lay a certain stress on the fact that Monsieur Rurange drank champagne with the Captain of the Port of Paita, and not record the circumstance of the parting glass and toast of his private Secretary, Lieutenant McInroy and Señor José Leon at Callao? The answer is obvious. Silence in two of the cases and communicativeness in the third, answered his purpose; but that purpose, malignant as it is, is too transparent to impose upon the serious and unprejudiced.

The narrative proceeds:

"A few hours before the departure of the "Talca," the Commodore observed on board a Peruvian vessel of war certain suspicious movements, and as he apprehended that some outrage might be attempted upon me, he offered me a guard of ten marines to carry me to Panama, an offer which I did not accept for considerations that your Excellency will easily appreciate. He then proceeded to the house of Rear-Admiral Valle-Riestra in company of the English Consul, when the latter declared in Spanish to the chief of the naval forces of Peru, on the part of the British naval authorities, that if any attempt were made against me on board the "Talca" he would seize every vessel of war belonging to the Republic, to which Señor Valle-Riestra replied by giving all kinds of assurances that nothing whatsoever should be attempted against me."

With respect to the above, I beg leave to observe that Señor Salazar's memory must be strangely defective if he indited the foregoing lines in good faith. I will, for his own sake, presume that his recollection is at fault, and, by a simple narration of facts, point out how incorrect is his version of the affair.

On the very evening to which he alludes, viz., the 13th of May, a little before sun-down, four persons on board H. B. Majesty's steam frigate "Leander" were dining in the cabin of Commodore Harvey. Those four persons were the Commodore himself, Eusebio de Salazar, Cecilio de Lora, and the writer of these lines.

The dinner had scarcely commenced when the steamer "Tumbes," under Peruvian colours, was seen entering the harbour of Callao, but, being met by a boat from the Peruvian flag-ship " Amazonas," she steamed out again.

The movements of this little vessel in an instant deprived Señor Salazar of all his good humour. He started up from his chair, turned pale, and after a few seconds reflection, addressing himself to Commodore Harvey, exclaimed that he had received notice that the steamer " Tumbes" was going to watch outside the harbour for the mail packet, in order to kidnap his own precious person.

It is therefore clear that this third charge which Señor Salazar raises against the Peruvian Government is totally incorrect. As it stands it not only makes a strong case against the authorities, but is an insinuation to the serious disadvantage of Commodore Harvey, who, as representing a power with which Peru was at peace, could have no right to interfere in matters that were foreign to his duty. Of course, if any violation of the English flag had taken place, the gallant Commodore could not, nor would he have hesitated a moment to use the forces at his command; but he observed none of those "suspicious movements" referred to " on board a Peruvian vessel of war;" the Peruvian fleet lay quietly at anchor under the guns of the fort; and the coming in and going out of the "Tumbes" was a matter so insignificant as to be almost unworthy of notice ; and I certainly should not have alluded to it, had not the wording of the Commissary's charge required the explanation.

With respect to the visit which the Commodore paid to Rear-Admiral Valle-Riestra, I may explain, by way of correction of Salazar's account of it, that Commodore Harvey considered it his duty to call on the Peruvian Rear-Admiral to mention to him the report which had thus reached his ears. That officer heard him with amazement depicted in his features, and assured the Commodore in reply that he was totally misinformed:—that the mission of the "Tumbes" was one of an ordinary, peaceful nature, and that under no circumstances would the British flag be violated. The Commodore, satisfied with this assurance, returned on board the "Leander," and explained to Señor Salazar that he run no risk whatsoever. Perceiving, however, that the Commissary still had misgivings, he offered him an escort of marines to protect him in case of danger. This proposal was refused, for it was obvious that if any mischief were intended on the part of a war steamer, a handful of soldiers could offer no effectual resistance.

Resolving then, after all, to confide in the good faith and plighted word of the Peruvian Rear-Admiral, Señor Salazar and suite embarked on board the "Talca" on the evening of the 13th of May.

The story thus goes on:—

"At seven precisely the said steamer weighed anchor, and coming alongside the "Leander," I passed on board, together with the gentlemen mentioned, Señores Lora and Cerruti. On the 14th I was advised by persons who were deserving of credit, to be very careful about my living, and as these same warnings were repeated on the 15th, I kept my cabin. One of the passengers, Mr. R—, the brother-in-law of a naval officer residing in Callao, endeavoured to gain my confidence, and I tried, through him, to obtain such data as I possibly could, respecting the intentions of the Peruvian Government regarding our squadron."

We find in the passage just quoted the same belief uppermost in Señor Salazar's mind, that not only was his life sought, but that the conspirators had used so little caution, that even indifferent persons were made acquainted with it. The supposition is so childish and improbable that it may with safety be left to the judgment of thinking men; but we cannot help noticing that in order to curry favour with the Minister to whom he addressed his letter, he thus publicly confesses that he did his best to pump from his casual acquaintance the secrets of the Peruvian authorities. It was unfortunate for the Special Commissary that he should on this occasion have made a confidant of a man who, not perhaps out of malice, but from that simple love of fun, which distinguishes his countrymen, "fooled him to the very top of his bent," and was only rejoiced at the opportunity thus offered to while away the tedium of a sea voyage.

This gentleman, whom Señor Salazar describes as Mr. R——, was a Captain Eugène Rurange, a French officer, who bore the decoration of the Cross of the Legion of Honour for bravery in the Crimean war, and could boast also of the possession of a large silver medal, bestowed on him by the Congress of the United States of America for his gallantry in rescuing the crew of an American whaling ship in distress. It was a peculiarity of Señor Salazar's to leave out the handle to the names of persons against whom he entertained any grudge, although he was diplomatically careful to append them to those of his friends.

Information as to the intentions of the Peruvian Government respecting the Spanish squadron or otherwise, he failed to obtain, and it may be said, in passing, that if he had succeeded in getting so-called "data," they could scarcely be considered reliable, viewing the quarter from whence they came.

I resume the narrative:

"On the morning of the 16th, Frank, the English steward who waited on me, confirmed the suspicions which had been awakened in my mind by other Spanish passengers (with whom he was not acquainted) observing: 'Take absolutely nothing but what I bring you, for one of the passengers,'—and he pointed out a person who, from the observation of Señors Lora and Cerruti, never ceased to dog my footsteps,—' Señor L——, a merchant, has just offered me 1000 dollars if I put a certain white powder into the cup of tea you take in the morning, 500 down, and the remainder at a later period; he says, it is only to throw you into a slumber so as to be able to get from you certain important papers you have got in your trunk. To this I answered, that I was an Englishman, a Christian, and an honest man, and that I would never lend myself to so infamous a transaction.' It is very evident that this powder was to do something more than merely send me to sleep, for as my two travelling companions never quitted my side, it was impossible to catch me alone. At night-fall, as the warnings were continued, we barricadoed ourselves in the cabin, piling our trunks against the door, and between that time and midnight, when all was perfectly dark, we heard some one trying the fastenings. Señor Lora immediately got up and heard the footsteps of some one gliding along the passage."

As regards this very romantic story I shall premise that not having been present when this honest English Christian made the foregoing revelation, I must pass it over in silence, but a little explanation may perhaps throw some light upon it, as also upon the other incidents of the narrative.

The attendant went to the Commissary's cabin on this occasion under the following circumstances. I had surprised him in close conversation with a gentleman who, as I fancied, was frequently watching Señor Salazar's movements. Calling him to me after his conference was over, I said: "Tom," (not *Frank*) "if anything happens to Mr. Salazar, I shall hold you responsible." He was stammering out some explanation, when I stopped him with the words: "If you have any declaration to make, go to the cabin and speak with Mr. Salazar himself."

He did so, and I had almost forgotten the occurrence, when, on arriving at Taboga, he told me that he had been offered a thousand dollars if he consented to put some morphine into the drink of his master.

This is all I know of the affair, and I therefore dismiss it, without other remark than that it would be absurd indeed to found on this reported revelation of a menial an accusation against the Peruvian Government or against a private individual.

Any way, before giving credence to it, it would be advisable to have the servant put upon his oath, and, in the presence of a magistrate, confronted with the merchant, Señor L——. By this means, one might perhaps arrive at the truth.

As to the passage of the story respecting the proposed abstraction of the papers and the barricading the cabin door at night, I must explain, that throughout this voyage, Señor Salazar was under the fixed persuasion that his life was to be attempted, and hence the singular precautions to which he alludes. It is true that some one *did* try the door, but so far from our (his companions) attaching any moment to the circumstance, we thought, as was doubtless the case, that in the darkness some one had made a mistake, and, on his discovering it, immediately moved away. To believe otherwise,—to believe that any single individual would attempt anything in a cabin occupied by three persons, two of them officers and armed,—surpasses ordinary credibility.

Señor Salazar continues :—

"On the 16th we reached Paita ; on board the steamer were various peasants and Peruvian officers who were to remain at that port ; two of them (one a naval officer) had formed the project of shooting me with their revolvers from a boat if I showed myself on deck. But they had discussed their plans with so little prudence that, through the passenger who occupied the adjoining cabin, it came to the ears of the Spanish actress, Dona Matilde Duclos, who was proceeding with her family to the Havana, so that, warned by her, I did not appear on deck until leaving Paita. This officer, by the peasants' statement, had said, 'If we get rid of Mazarredo, we will give you a deal of money, and they will promote me to the rank of Captain of Corvette.'"

I can readily conceive the astonishment which an Englishman, who is accustomed in all matters of accusation to look for the proofs with which they are supported, will feel at such loose statements as the foregoing being uttered by a public diplomatic official, and received by a Minister of State as good evidence against the accused! If we are to take as gospel all these wondrous revelations, which crowd upon us more thickly than in the tales that are dished up for the especial consumption of the readers of some of the penny journals, we must believe that the Peruvian Government is so unscrupulous that it stops at no measures to be rid of a disagreeable adversary, and that the Peruvian people are so degraded that tools are to be found among all classes ready to commit the basest of crimes.

Would it not be thought the proper course for a gentleman in Señor Salazar's position to prove by means of affidavits, or other binding forms, the serious charges which he brings, and openly publishes to the world ? And, if he cannot so substantiate them, to suppress them altogether ? Is it sufficient to thrust them thus publicly forward upon the mere report of individuals, designated by initials; and is he justified, even supposing his facts to be as he states them, in laying these charges at the door of the authorities of Peru, because, to use his own words, he left no private enemies in the country?

Comment on the foregoing passage of the narrative would seem superfluous if the Spanish Minister, Señor Pacheco, had not allowed it to pass muster, and were not apparently disposed to support both that and kindred assertions with such powerful arguments as iron-plated steamers and other paraphernalia of war.

Concluding, therefore, that the incidents alluded to must be of greater worth than I should otherwise have attached to them, I must express my regret that Señor Salazar has suppressed the name of that gallant naval officer who aspired to be promoted to the rank of "Captain of Corvette," if he were fortunate enough to put an end to the career of the Special Commissary. For the information of the public I can inform them that there was but *one* Peruvian naval officer on board the "Talca" on the occasion alluded to, and, if I am not mistaken, he was a deputy of the Captain of the Port at Paita.

And will Señor Salazar or Mlle. Duclos kindly inform us who the passenger was whose cabin adjoined that of the conspirators, and who overheard and reported their conversation?

To resume :—

"I thought that my adventures were to terminate here, and scarce thought it necessary to observe the ordinary behaviour of the passengers, but it really was but the beginning of them. M. R—— feigned, when at Paita,—no doubt with a view to inspire me with confidence,—that the Captain of the Port was desirous of seizing him ; and then, after a scene where much talk and insulting language were used, sat down quietly to drink champagne with the authorities of the town ;—a proceeding which was not very calculated to induce me to fall into his nets."

This is another of the numerous instances of misrepresentation of facts to suit a purpose to which I have more than once had occasion to allude as a distinguishing feature of Señor Salazar's narrative.

The Captain of the Port did not merely *feign* to arrest M. R—, but did in fact arrest him and bring him on board the steamer bound for Panamá; and he moreover put a guard over him to prevent his returning to Callao. The motives which induced the Captain of the Port to take this step, would have justified him in adopting still harsher ones ; and if I do not here reveal them, the Special Commissary ought to feel grateful for my silence.

As to the champagne which was drunk on the occasion, I cannot but admire Señor Salazar's ingenuity in thus wresting from a simple incident a meaning of so significant a kind.

It happened that among the passengers was a kindly tempered gentleman, by name Miró Quesada, who having a great dislike to squabbles, and wishing to obliterate from memory the disagreeable scene of the arrest, invited the Captain of the Port, M. R—, and several of the passengers to take wine with him. They consented and drank, and Señor Quesada paid the score. What comes then of all this story of manœuvres "to inspire confidence," and danger to personal safety?

The narrative continues:—

"I learnt indirectly through this gentleman the contents of a letter which I had written the day previous to Don Mariano Prado, our Chargé d'Affaires at Quito; it was entrusted to the Clerk of the steamer, and notwithstanding that it was in a double envelope for the English Consul at Guayaquil, it was opened by the Post Office authorities at Paita. Fortunately I had put nothing in it that was of importance."

This charge is as serious as it is sweeping. It raises a doubt as to the integrity of the Purser of the steamer (who was not a Peruvian), and openly attacks the Post Office officials at Paita, thus raising a feeling of distrust throughout the community of South America as to the safety of their correspondence; for it must be borne in mind that all the mails from Europe to Ecuador, Bolivia, Chili, and Peru pass through the hands of the agents referred to. But *can* this story be true? Would one single quarter of an hour,—the time that the passengers remained on shore,—suffice for the contents of Señor Salazar's letter to be made known?

The narrative runs on:—

"There was on board the "Talca" a Frenchman, who, desirous of paying but little for his passage, had offered himself, as was frequently the case, to serve at the passengers' table. On the eve of reaching Panamá, he came to inform me that the said M. R— had desired him to bring a small bottle of ale to his cabin, where he said to him, 'I have remarked that Señor Salazar takes a bottle just like this at his dinner; if you give him this, after putting into it a white powder (showing a paper packet), I will make you a present of 300 dollars down.' The Frenchman, instead of accepting the proposal, related the occurrence to several of the passengers. Directly I heard of it, being unable to restrain my anger, I called M. R—, shut him up in his own cabin, and had my suspicions confirmed by the mode in which he replied to the unmeasured terms in which I accused him. He excused himself in a miserable way, and with faltering aspect drank the contents of the bottle before me to prove his innocence. I complained to the Captain of the steamer, who corroborated the rumours which had reached my ears as to the intentions of certain Peruvians, and we were both of opinion that a formal plaint should be made before the French Consul at Panamá, as R— had had plenty of time to get rid of the evidence of his intended crime. I must mention here that both the man Frank, and the Frenchman alluded to, enjoy the best reputation."

Señor Salazar appears in the foregoing exciting incident, in quite a novel character. Hitherto, we have observed him wonderfully careful of his person; according to his own confession, very unwilling to appear on deck as a mark for aspiring naval officers to fire at, and barricading his cabin with portmanteaus to prevent the entrance of midnight purloiners and assassins. But on this occasion, we find him acting with an energy that is quite startling; —shutting himself up alone in Captain Rurange's cabin, and compelling that gentleman to go through a little private performance to prove his innocence, while he assails him in the most "unmeasured terms."

I can say nothing about the truth of a story which had but two actors,—one of them the narrator,—and no spectators; but I refuse to give it credence, because I find one of the premises to be false. The M. R— alluded to had no cabin of his own, and therefore could not be shut up in it. His sleeping place was in the after saloon, where he occupied a berth with Messrs. Galesi, a Peruvian doctor, whose name has escaped me, and two others. All those gentlemen had paid first-class fare and were therefore entitled to cabins, but the steamer "Talca" being a small vessel, several of the first-class passengers were compelled to sleep in the dining saloon, and others, as I have stated, in the after saloon.

But what are we to think of the passage referring to Captain Galloway, the gentleman in command of the steamer, who, responsible as he is for the safety of his passengers, allowed rumours of attempts to be made on Señor Salazar's life without an effort to inquire into or stay them; and says not a word of their being afloat, until the Special Commissary broaches the subject? This is a grave charge, and it behoves Captain Galloway to clear his reputation of it, lest his silence be misconstrued. By coming forward, either to corroborate or refute this declaration of Señor Salazar, he will be doing a public service, and if I judge him correctly he will not fail to do so when this romantic story shall reach his ears.

It is a singular fact that although the Special Commissary insists upon accusing Peru,—her government and people,—of these continued attempts upon his life, and has induced his superior, Señor Pacheco, to coincide with his views, he has, up to this point of his narrative, brought upon the scene as the intended assassins, Frenchmen, Englishmen, any countrymen but Peruvians. The Señor L— for instance is a Canadian; M. R— is a Frenchman; and the two men in attendance are English and French respectively. Is it at all likely that the Peruvian Government, if bent on taking Señor Salazar's life, should have used foreign agents for such a purpose?

With respect to the Commissary's assurance that both the attendant, Frank, and the Frenchman enjoyed the best reputation, I can only say as regards the former, that if he did enjoy such reputation, he did not deserve it. His honesty may be judged from the fact that he was paid at Taboga by Señor Emilio Galesi, the sum of four dollars, partly in requital of his service and partly as prepayment for the removal of the trunks of his (Señor Galesi's) sick cousin. Honest Frank pocketed the money with a christian spirit of contentment, but failed to perform the duty for which it was part consideration.

The tale then proceeds as follows :—

"We reached that port in the afternoon of the 20th, and I walked about the town, accompanied by the French Consul, Mr. Zeltner, without meeting with any molestation. We fell in with the Frenchman whom they had attempted to suborn to poison me, and he made a full declaration before the Consul. A short time after, we learnt that a Peruvian, an employé of the tailoring establishment at Callao, in connection with the State Navy, and the travelling companion of M. R—, had struck him before one of the hotels for having denounced his friend. The Frenchman came to make his complaint, and Mr. Zeltner summoned him for the following day."

As I know most positively that the employé or clerk to whom allusion is here made, is not a Peruvian but an European, I at once call attention to the mistake, for it would ill-accord with the Peruvians' repute for "mildness of character," to find them thus, on the slightest provocation, brawling in the public streets. Señor Salazar's account too of the quarrel, is not, as I am informed, quite the correct one.

It would appear that the Clerk, a Mr. L—, had high words with the French servant of excellent reputation, because, when at Panamá, he denied having said anything against M. R—. Whilst they were disputing, a certain Gomez, a diamond merchant, came up, and positively declared that the Frenchman had accused M. R— of intending to poison Señor Salazar, and asserted that he had brought the charge in the expectation of reaping a good reward.

This asseveration of Gomez' led, after some more words, to blows, but the whole affair was over in a few minutes,—none of the parties receiving any serious hurt.

With regard to the summons for the following day, I can only observe that if there were any intention to issue it, such resolve was never carried out, for the simple reason that Mr. Zeltner left Panamá for Aspinwall at half-past four in the morning. But, suppose he had issued it, what result could it have led to, since, as Señor Salazar assures the Minister, the assaulting party was a Peruvian? What authority can the French Consul at Panamá exercise over Peruvian subjects?

I transcribe Señor Salazar's words in continuation :—

"The seizure of the Islands, known twenty days previously, had not occasioned any great stir at this place; on the contrary, when General Herran, who had emigrated to Peru, arrived by the previous packet, charged with a commission from the Government of Lima to purchase munitions of war in the United States, the authorities ordered the troops to be put under arms, directly they heard of his coming, and opposed his crossing the Isthmus."

The reader will observe that the Spanish Special Commissary thus complacently attributes to a feeling of consideration of the people of Panamá towards himself, the steps thus taken against General Herran. But the motives of such measures were of a perfectly different kind. General Herran was known to be opposed to the actual state of affairs, and it was also known that his influence in New Granada, where he had held the post of Minister, was so great, that his presence only was needed to light the torch of civil war in that country. The whole statement is a garbled one; for General Herran was bound to California on this occasion, and not to the United States; and the authorities could not be said to prevent his crossing the Isthmus when he had no intention of doing so.

The story continues :—

"At night-fall, General Iriarte, formerly Commandant General of Panamá, whose acquaintance I had made on board the "Resolucion" months before, came to inform me that he had learnt from a safe quarter that something disagreeable was hatching against me, and that he thought I had better push on to Colon. M. de Zeltner and the English Consul, Mr. Henderson, called at once upon the Governor of the State; but his servant replied that he was not at home. Commodore Harvey and Mr. Jerningham, the English Minister at Lima, had given me letters of recommendation from Mr. Petrie, the General Agent of the Pacific Steam Navigation Company to his private agent in Panamá. This gentleman transferred the recommendation to Mr. Nelson, Superintendent of the Isthmus Railway, who displayed his kindness, when he heard what had passed, by lodging me in his own house, 'because,' he said, 'no one would believe that the Minister of Spain had taken refuge in the dwelling of the representative of a North American Company, when European Consuls placed their residences at his disposal.'"

The above passage was doubtless written with the object of contrasting the reception of General Herran with the one accorded to himself; for as, in the one case, he describes nothing but hostility and menace, in the other he brings forward the most puerile details in order to exhibit the anxiety to render service. Myself and others put a different construction upon General Iriarte's attentions. Knowing full well the excitable nature of the Panamá populace, composed as it is of a most miscellaneous character, he was apprehensive of so strong a "bone of contention" as Her Catholic Majesty's Special Commissary making any stay in the place, and therefore used every means to get him speedily out of the way.

The narrative proceeds :—

"In fact, at half-past ten at night there assembled before the French Consulate from thirty to forty negroes, followed by as many boys, who uttered the strangest cries, and made a horrible noise with all sorts of implements. This uproar being over they went away, but before twelve the negroes came back and called out 'Death to Spain! Death to the Queen! Down with France! the Emperor! General Pinzon and myself!' They then smashed the windows of the Consulate; they injured the Imperial Arms, and would have torn down the flag which M. de Zeltner had ordered to be put out when the tumult began, if a person who was with them had not called out, 'No, no; don't touch the flag,' when they retired, contenting themselves with pelting it with dirt. I was an ear-witness to these scenes from the house of Mr. Nelson; and when they were over, the French and English Consuls came in, and it was resolved that M. de Zeltner, Señor Lora and myself, should leave at four in the morning for Paraiso,—the name of a station on the railway about eight miles distant from Panamá."

Señor Salazar here endeavours to convert a paltry demonstration on the part of a ragged mob, who seemed as much moved by fun as mischief, into one of political significance. He says he heard all that passed from Mr. Nelson's house; but he describes things which required also a little ocular demonstration to make them valuable as evidence; otherwise he must repeat them on hearsay; now I both saw and heard the whole affair, and I assert that, to my knowledge, *no* windows were smashed and *no* injury done to the Imperial arms of France. The mob, too, must have had long arms if they intended pulling down the flag, for it happened to be flying at the top of the house. There is some inaccuracy, also, in the Commissary's record of the cries that were uttered. I did not hear them shout "Death to the Emperor!" or "Death to General Pinzon!" But I *did* hear them exclaim, "Long live Pinzon!" which I attributed to the fact that during that gentleman's stay at Panamá in the month of November last year, he had endeared himself to the townspeople by many acts of kindness. Señor Salazar suppresses, and for obvious reasons, the cry that was most predominant of all, viz., "Death to the truce of 40 years!" The recording such a circumstance might have read as an uncomfortable commentary on that principle of "revindication" which was promulgated on the 14th of April, with the seizure of the Chincha Islands; and he therefore perhaps deemed it most prudent to suppress it.

His story follows on thus :—

"Mr. Nelson gave me the two annexed letters, numbered 1 and 2, for the chief official of the station at Panamá, Señor Diaz, and for the station-master at Paraiso, Mr. Hughes; but after mature reflection, he preferred accompanying us himself in the vehicle that was to convey us to the station. This was a hand-car, uncovered, which, moved by two men by means of a species of mechanism, can run upon rails at the rate of seven or eight miles an hour. On reaching the station, Mr. Nelson said to me: 'I will give you two confidential negroes who will accompany you to Paraiso. You will there wait for the train which brings the treasure from California (*the specie train*), and by this means avoid all annoyance. I have the telegraph at my disposal, and will give orders to prevent any suspicious message from being transmitted.' Señor Diaz added, that during the night several negroes had gone along the line, and advised us to proceed with great care. We got our pistols in readiness, and in little more than an hour reached the appointed place, in the midst of a storm which wetted us completely through, although it is not improbable it may have saved us from something worse than a wetting."

The foregoing extract contains a good deal of matter of a perfectly indifferent character, and as it does not bear upon the question at issue may be dismissed with a few passing words. The party of travellers were of course justified in taking such precautions for their personal safety as they considered the gravity of their position required; and not even Señor Salazar, who can scent out a plot with almost as keen a nose as King Jamie himself, of glorious memory, will attempt to prove that the wetting which he publicly records was specially designed by the Peruvian Government to make him uncomfortable. He however perhaps holds that it was sent by a special Providence to guard him from the machinations of his enemies, for he observes that " it is not improbable it may have saved us from something worse than a wetting."

But the words which Señor Salazar puts into the mouth of Mr. Nelson, if correctly reported, make that gentleman liable to a serious charge. The telegraph is a public institution, established under certain conditions, it is for the use of the public, and no official having it under his control, is justified in making it an instrument for the exclusive advantage of any private individual. The story is a doubtful one; but under any circumstances, the freedom with which the Special Commissary compromises persons in responsible positions in order to make out his own case, is an ugly peculiarity which will not escape the attention of the reader.

He then proceeds :—

" At Paraiso I conceived the happy idea of continuing on instead of stopping; we changed our negroes, and resting every four miles arrived at Colon (Aspinwall) at a quarter to one. Immediately on my alighting, the station-master handed to me the annexed telegram, marked 3, to the effect that Mr. Nelson had refused to allow several very suspicious messages from going forward. Mr. Nelson was under the impression that we should start from Paraiso by the specie train. By that train, the employé of the tailoring establishment at Callao had in fact crossed the Isthmus, and as I was informed afterwards, on board the steamer by Mr. Madellan (the master of one of the intermediate stations), he had exhibited the utmost surprise and annoyance when he learnt that I must be already on board the " Solent." I may here observe that the speed with which we traversed the forty-eight miles freed us from other danger; for as Mr. Nelson was not aware of our having continued on by the hand carriage, he had given no notice to the guard of the train, and it would have been very easy for us to have been run down by the one conveying the specie.

"The train that followed brought on M. R—— with a party of negroes wretchedly attired, armed with chopping-knives and revolvers. On reaching Paraiso, where they expected to fall in with me, they sought for me in every direction. They then took counsel and decided upon going on. They were seen in the train, in one of the carriages (an American one, holding forty passengers), by Sir Greville Smythe, Bart., Captain Paul, M. Daignoux, one of the proprietors of the Hotel Aspinwall at Panamá, M. Léon Plaus de Couteret, M. Peyroux de Pontacq, Messieurs Fontanilly, Riembasc and others, foreigners and Spaniards. Of the latter I shall subsequently speak. As to the foreigners, they assured me that if the negroes had fallen in with me, there would have been a terrible struggle, for all were disposed to take up my defence."

Passing over, in my comments on the foregoing extract, the mysterious re-appearance *somewhere* on the road, of the tailors' clerk, who, according to Mr. Madellan, gave vent to his surprise and annoyance at having missed the Special Commissary, I am bound to express my sympathy at the awful danger run by Señor Salazar of being crushed by a train which did not arrive at Aspinwall *until he had been five hours at least on board the Solent!* My feelings are modified by the reflection, that, as he had a *nine hours'* start of the specie train, and as the distance to be run over was only forty-eight miles, the peril he encountered was not very imminent after all. He is correct in stating that a suspicious party of negroes came on by that train; but not so in the assertion that on reaching Paraiso they "sought about for him in every direction." The train only stopped *about one or two minutes* in that place, and had any of the passengers wandered away, they would most certainly have been left behind. Señor Salazar instances certain persons who observed the negroes, but one among them at least, M. Daignoux, could not have seen them. That gentleman was at Panamá at the very time referred to, and did not arrive at Aspinwall till half-past seven that night, having come on by a slow train.

Señor Salazar then proceeds:—

"The negroes and the two emissaries came up as far as the very wharf where the steamer was moored. The Captain of the "Solent," for whom the English Consul in Panamá had given me a letter, and his officers ordered them off; but the emissaries managed to come on board. M. R—— even succeeded in speaking to me, and begged that I would intercede with the French Consul so as to prevent any further proceedings; he said that the Frenchman withdrew his charge and other things of a similar kind; to this I replied before Mr. Zeltner, 'The French Consul will do what he may consider advisable.'"

Señor Salazar here asserts that the Captain of the "Solent," together with his officers, drove away from the wharf the negroes who, armed as he has described, had travelled from Panamá to Aspinwall for the purpose of taking his life.

Will the Captain of the "Solent" and his officers make an affidavit to that effect, and declare that they did so because they were of opinion that the ragged band meant mischief to the Spanish Commissary's person? If so, it will give a colour of truth to this assertion. By Señor Salazar's own showing, they could not keep out the ringleaders, for they actually forced their way on board and had speech of the envoy.

And what are the proceedings to which he alludes? None certainly had as yet been taken, and how could they be initiated or gone on with in the absence of the prosecutor? The whole is a tissue of contradictions; for if the Frenchman alluded to had retracted his supposititious charge there did not even remain a witness against M. R——.

Again, are Aspinwall and Panamá French Colonies that the Consul of the Empire is to do "what *he* may consider advisable" in the matter? Besides, had not Señor Salazar himself spoken to the friendly feeling towards him of General Iriarte and many other parties in Panamá, both officials and private individuals, and were not they much more likely—were they not indeed the parties to take up the affair rather than the French Consul?

But what becomes of the statement of the Special Commissary when I assert, as I unhesitatingly do, that it was at Señor Salazar's request, made to Messrs. R—— and L—— through me, his private Secretary, that those gentlemen went on board the "Solent" to have an interview with him? What passed at that interview I cannot, of course, reveal; but as the manner in which it was brought about is incorrectly stated, no great value can be attached to the Spanish envoy's revelation of what took place at it.

He then goes on:—

"On board the steamer, the North American Consul at Colon,

Mr. Mac Rice, presented himself to me and offered his services under these critical circumstances.

"A short time afterwards, the Callao employé approached the Spanish bullfighter Marin, who was proceeding with us in order to cross from St. Thomas to the Havana. Marin knew him to be from Peru, assailed him in the strongest terms of abuse, and if I had not interfered, he would have knocked him down on board the steamer. Both he and R—— confessed to Marin that the scene at Paita was a regular comedy, and that they had obtained some 2000 dollars and had the promise of 20,000 more if they succeeded in getting possession of my papers. That is to say, that it was the story of the steamer "Talca" continued. But were so many armed negroes required for such a purpose? Should I have allowed my papers to be taken from me? And what would have been the result of the struggle which must have ensued?"

So we find from this strange story, Messrs. L—— and R——, those redoubted chieftains, at length coming out in their true colours, and, honest for once, actually confessing the part they had taken in the foregoing persecution, and the reward they were to receive if successful in it. But to whom do they make the revelation? Is it to some Father of the Church, who by the ecclesiastical laws is a safe depositary of human secrets? By no means. The avowal is made to an erring mortal like themselves, a Spanish *Bullfighter!* Doubtless, it was the indignation caused by this confession of their villainy which roused the *Torero* to such a pitch as to almost knock them down on the deck of the steamer, although Señor Salazar reverses the order and makes them quarrel first, and be boon companions afterwards; with a man too of the lowest class, as his occupation betrays, and who was indebted to Señor Salazar's own bounty for the very journey he was taking.

Seriously, how comes it that I, who was on board the vessel, and had the actors of the singular scenes thus described constantly in sight, knew nothing of this quarrel until the appearance of Señor Salazar's letter? And yet, if Marin had been concerned in it, and had carried it on to the point alluded to, where words, namely, are about to give way to blows, I could scarcely have been ignorant of the fact, or indeed any individual on board,—for of all the noisy fellows I ever fell in with, Master Marin was about the most boisterous.

It is a thousand pities that the confession about the money part of the transaction should be so meagre, for could Señor Salazar have boldly asserted *who* it was that advanced the 2000 dollars in cash, and was to advance the 20,000 more, it would have saved a vast amount of conjecture, and prevented the suspicion being cast perhaps upon the wrong parties. It stands as an isolated and doubtful assertion, and I shall greatly err, if thinking men will in its present shape attach the slightest weight to it.

To resume the narrative :—

"In spite of everything, the employé referred to did not consider that his mission was at an end, and it came to our knowledge that he intended to take a ticket for Southampton. M. Zeltner, however, observed aloud, 'This man last night ill-treated a French subject, and I shall resolutely oppose his embarkation.' As soon as this threat reached his ears, he quietly went off to join his negroes, who kept within pistol-shot of the steamer; not without, however, previously exclaiming that if I came ashore, he would blow my brains out.

"On board the steamer I received a letter from a Spanish merchant established at Panamá, advising me of the journey of the negroes and their intentions. I cannot find it among my papers, but Señor Garcia is very well known there.

"The authorities of the Isthmus did nothing to prevent their excesses, and I have, upon this point, written likewise to the Captain-General of the Island of Cuba. The head of the police at Panamá, when accused for his indifference, replied, 'that if he quarrelled with those few negroes, there was reason to fear that all the others would make common cause with them, and that the result might be as fatal as the *émeute* which occurred a few years back, and that cost many North Americans their lives.'"

Passing over in the foregoing extract the extraordinary authority with which M. Zeltner is invested by our Special Commissary, I cannot help expressing my admiration at the boldness of the man, who, in order to pleasure his protégé, thus beards the ringleader of a band of negroes, armed as we have seen, and who were within pistol shot of the steamer, ready to answer his call!

With respect to Señor Garcia, to whom he alludes, and whose wonderful power of divination in penetrating the *intentions* of the negroes is not obscurely hinted at, I cannot forget that Señor Salazar did not always speak of him so politely. The using his name in the way in which it appears in this extract, is another proof of how little the Spanish envoy is stayed by any scruples when he has a purpose to serve. He is right in stating that Garcia is well known at Panamá:—perhaps better known than trusted. Does Señor Salazar forget how that worthy gentleman charged him 540 reals, or £5. 10s. sterling, for merely forwarding a small trunk and hat box from Panamá to Aspinwall?

The Spanish Commissary is unjustly severe upon the Chief of the Police at Panamá for his so-called indifference to the *charivari* at that place, when we all passed through it. His reply, even as reported by Señor Salazar, was by no means an unreasonable one. That functionary had but thirty-two men at his disposal, and as he saw the mob contenting itself with empty noise he very wisely refrained from interference. If our Special Commissary had only possessed a little of the discretion displayed by the Panamá Police Officer, and which he is so ready to condemn, it is just possible that the present hostile attitude between two kindred nations might have been avoided.

"These are in simple form," observes Señor Salazar in conclusion, "the facts of the case. From St. Thomas I wrote to the Captain-General of Cuba to draw up an official account of the affair. At the Havana, whither proceeded Señor Lora and various Spaniards, viz. the actors Ortiz and Duclos, the bullfighter Marin, a Banderillero (flag carrier in bull fights) whose name I do not remember, and others to the number of ten, proper declarations will have been made by those parties."

It is to be hoped so. It is most desirable that proper declarations should be made; but one would have thought that the Minister of Spain would wait till some such documentary evidence came forward before so readily endorsing a narrative whose puerilities and reckless assertions are patent to every attentive reader.

The narrative of Señor Salazar winds up as follows:—

"In view of the foregoing, it is evident that my life has been saved by a miracle, and I believe that Her Majesty's Government will be doing an act of justice by expressing its thanks to Commodore Harvey of the English Navy, to the Superintendent of the Isthmus Railway, Mr. Nelson, to the Consuls, Messrs. Zeltner, Henderson, and MacRice, for the support given by them to its representative; and such thanks are more especially due to the French Consul, as he ran serious danger in performing the act of abnegation of which I have made mention.

"I will close this despatch with one simple reflection; that I have not left in Lima any personal enemies. The expense occasioned by the wicked attempts referred to, must have been very considerable, for the mere crossing of the Isthmus costs 500 reals a head, and as it is scarcely to be supposed that patriotic enthusiasm against my humble person could assume such proportions, I may be permitted to ask, 'Who was interested in the committal of such attempts? And who, feeling such interest, could have incurred so vast an outlay?'"

The conclusion at which Señor Salazar wishes us to arrive is obvious. As he asserts that he had no *personal* enemies in Lima, and yet his life was in imminent danger from poison, the bullet, and the chopping knife, from the moment of his quitting it until he stood beneath the flag of England bound for its shores, his would-be assassins must be *public* ones, must in fact be emissaries of the Peruvian Government, who alone,—as he carefully insinuates,—could have borne the expense.

The reader must decide, after a perusal of the Spanish envoy's letter (which I have, although in detached portions, transcribed in its entirety) and the light which my personal knowledge has been able to throw upon it, what credence should be given to these heavy charges against the authorities of Peru.

It is natural to suppose that a man whose insulting words had wounded the pride of an entire nation, and whose unscrupulous deed had just deprived the Republic of one of the main sources of her revenue, would not meet with particular courtesy at the hands of the Peruvians who happened to cross his path; it is also not improbable that some of the more unscrupulous among them would have done him a mischief if they had found the opportunity; but it is base to endeavour by such assertions as I have exposed to cast a stigma upon a whole people, and most wicked by such insidious accusations to raise to a still higher pitch the angry feelings already excited.

The more, however, one reflects upon the matter, the greater becomes the hope of a pacific solution to the present difficulties. It cannot be that the act of a man, capable of inditing such a tissue of misrepresentations as is here set forth, will be permitted to plunge whole nations into all the horrors of war. The idea is too preposterous to be entertained; common sense forbids it; and although in the course of this unhappy dispute, it is a commodity that has been very sparingly used, I still believe, as I do most fervently pray, that it will ultimately prevail.

POSTSCRIPT.—Before closing these pages, I cannot refrain from laying before my readers a letter which appeared on the 14th of July in one of the official organs of Madrid; " El Eco del Pais," to which Señor Salazar y Mazarredo is a contributor. The effusion will at least confirm what I have before stated, viz. the utter recklessness with which assertions are made, when a purpose has to be served or a spite to be vented. It is fortunate in productions like the present that the cunning with which they are composed is inferior to the venom that they contain, and that their very *animus* almost invariably betrays their worthlessness.

" Panamá, 20th June, 1864.

" On the steamer ' Chile ' arriving off Pisco (Peru), there came on board, requesting a passage to Panamá, two officers of the Spanish squadron in the Pacific; their request was immediately complied with.

" Those passengers were Don José Oreyro, second commander of the Spanish frigate ' Resolucion,' and the other an officer also of the Spanish navy. Señor Oreyro at once, in presence of witnesses, and with the greatest *solemnity* possible in such cases, delivered to the Captain of the steamer " Chile," a well closed bag, sealed with red wax, bearing a clear impress of the arms of France, the bag itself being addressed to the French Consul at Panamá.

" On delivering this bag, Señor Oreyro said that it contained the Official Correspondence between France and Spain, that he wished it to be put into the iron safe, so as to prevent any risk of its being stolen, and kept and conveyed under his (the Captain's) responsibility. Captain Sivell took the bag and had it stored in the iron safe; in a word, the correspondence between Spain and France was deposited in the hands of an English Admiralty Agent on board a ship of war of Great Britain.

" In the afternoon of the 19th of June, the steamer arrived in the Bay of Panamá, and before any of the passengers landed, Señor Oreyro asked Captain Sivell for the bag containing the correspondence which he had consigned to his care in the Bay of Pisco. The Captain ordered the Purser to deliver up the bag, which he did at once, without the slightest remark; but on receiving it, Señor Oreyro observed that the seal had been broken and half covered with common wax, the cord which closed the bag had been removed, the correspondence stolen and its place supplied with blank letters and envelopes, addressed to various parties in Spain and France.

" The Captain, instead of preventing any one from going ashore before reporting the matter to H. B. Majesty's Consul or to either of the Commanders of the two English war vessels which were lying at anchor near him, allowed the passengers to land and took no steps whatsoever to clear the honour of Great Britain.

" The Purser endeavours to exonerate himself by saying that without doubt the theft was committed in Callao, but no one believes this, not even the Purser himself. On board the ' Chile' there embarked at Callao and came on to Panamá on the 19th June, two persons, worthy servants of Peru (judging them by their deeds), and unfortunately well known to Señor Don Eusebio Salazar y Mazarredo, against whom, as all the world knows, they plotted at Panamá and Colon, in the month of May.

" Those two individuals, Juan Noguier and Eugène Ruveran, are French renegades. According to their confidential reports, the assertions of their friends and private letters from Lima, they are commissioned by the Peruvian Government, especially to steal official correspondence, to persecute diplomats wherever they may fall in with them, and who knows what more!

" In conclusion, the Purser of the ' Chile' is a Peruvian, and Captain Sivell is married in Lima."

The writer of this precious epistle doubtless fancies that the inference to be drawn from the concluding remark will be a clincher; but what must be the state of a cause which is attempted to be bolstered up by silly letters such as these?

Any way, the composition is well worthy of its author, whether it be written by Monsieur Zeltner, as the "Espiritu Publico" seems to think, or by his whilom protégé Señor Eusebio de Salazar.

Its origin, and the origin of many others published at the same time, is clearly this. The famous despatch of the 20th June, which we have recently taken occasion to analyse, required some collateral support, and it is obtained by the insertion of this and similar letters in the Spanish journals.

"*Dans le pays des aveugles, les borgnes sont rois!*" says the old proverb, and true it is, that the mass of readers must necessarily be so ignorant of matters occurring at distant points of the globe and of the localities where they are enacted, that it becomes comparatively easy for those who have but a trifling knowledge to impose upon them. They cannot, however, deceive the initiated; and when I turn to the letter in question I find an error at the very outset. Don José Oreyro was *not* second commander of the "Resolucion;" the gentleman who holds that position being Don Pedro Ossa y Geraldo, an officer of distinction and promise. The name of Oreyro nowhere appears upon the frigate's books, and no officer of that name proceeding from the flag-ship of the Spanish Pacific squadron could have embarked at Pisco.

Passing this over, however, I come upon a passage which betrays the romance writer by profession. The circumstantiality of the description and the solemn way in which the subject is introduced and the reader prepared for something mysterious and strange, are in their way not devoid of cleverness:—

"Señor Oreyro at once, in presence of witnesses, and with the greatest solemnity possible in such cases, delivered to the Captain of the steamer 'Chile' a well-closed bag, sealed with red wax, bearing a clear impress of the arms of France; the bag itself being addressed to the French Consul at Panamá."

But why the arms of France, since the bag was supposed to contain the despatches of the Spanish authorities, and was being conveyed by a Spanish official? Scarcely do we learn that the Imperial Arms were sacrilegiously defaced, and Frenchmen thereby made to feel uneasy at the audacity of some party or parties unknown, but pretty clearly hinted at a little farther on, than England comes in for her share of insult, as thus: "The correspondence of Spain and France was deposited in the hands of an English Admiralty Agent on board a ship of war of Great Britain."

Unfortunately for the veracity of the writer, every person who, of late years, has travelled from Valparaiso to Panamá, is aware that there is no Admiralty Agent in the Pacific, and that under no circumstances is a mail-bag transferred to an English vessel of war. But what has the author of this tissue of calumnies and absurdities to do with truth? Is he not at least fully acquainted with the correctness of the doctrine, "Throw plenty of mud, and some of it is sure to stick," and does he not thoroughly act up to it ? His story goes on to say, that "when the steamer arrived in the Bay of Panamá, and before any of the passengers landed, Señor Oreyro asked Captain Sivell for the bag, &c." In order to understand what a wonderful feat this Señor Oreyro here performed, it is necessary to know that the " Chile," on account of her draught of water, or some other cause, does not go further than Taboga; on this occasion, however, most probably with a view "to point a moral and adorn *this* tale," she is made to go up to Panamá !

The authorship of the epistle peeps out in unmistakeable terms in the concluding paragraphs, for not only the style of the composition, but the unscrupulous use of slanderous assertions, indicates that the famous Despatch is own brother to the letter under review. But why, I would ask, is our old acquaintance M. R——, and whom I have before described to be Captain Ruverange, converted into Eugène Ruveran? And why does another old acquaintance, formerly introduced to us as M. L —— now assume a different cognomen?

But I am ashamed to continue the critical examination of a document which would be beneath contempt if the malice which dictated it and the great interests that it helps to imperil did not give it and similar productions an undue weight. I have done enough, however, to enable those who wish to judge with fairness to form an unbiassed opinion ; and if I were to fill volumes with commentaries I could scarcely hope to succeed in convincing those whose minds are clouded by prejudice and passion.

APPENDIX.

I.

The following extract of the circular of Señor Pacheco, the Spanish Minister for Foreign Affairs, to the Representatives of Her Catholic Majesty at Foreign Courts, dated Madrid, the 24th of June, 1864, will be perused with interest, as being the document which accompanied the despatch of Señor Salazar y Mazarredo, already analysed:—

"I need not speak to your Excellency either of the agitation which has been excited by the above-mentioned incidents, both in Peru and in other parts of America, nor of the unsuccessful steps taken by several of the diplomatic agents resident in Lima, intended to bring that Government to an agreement with Señores Pinzon and Salazar. With regard to those steps, Her Majesty's Government is grateful for them, although they have not produced any effect; with regard to the agitation, as it was chiefly caused by the idea that it was to revindicate ancient rights, it was natural, and it is natural, that it should have been calmed, or that it will be calmed, so soon as it shall be known in America that Spain and her Government did not admit, but rather had disapproved, such revindication.

"But I have now to inform you of a matter still more unexpected by us than the rejection of our agent, and which I do not intend to designate. I mean the voyage to Spain undertaken by Señor Salazar, and I refer to the deplorable circumstances which attended it, from the waters of Peru to the passage across the Isthmus of Panamá and the arrival at Colon.

"What occurred in the voyage to which I allude, your Excellency will find related *in extenso* in the despatch of Señor Salazar himself, copy of which I enclose. It would be useless to repeat it, and I therefore confine myself to a recapitulation thereof in a few words.

"In the port of Callao, an armed force, with orders from the Peruvian authorities, endeavoured to take possession of the Secretary of Señor Salazar, who was on board of an English vessel.

"From the very port of Callao to Paita (Peru) first, afterwards to Panamá, and lastly to Colon or Aspinwall, Señor Salazar was accompanied and followed by certain Peruvians, who, now by means of poison, and now by other modes, endeavoured to put an end to his life.

"Of the first of those two acts—the attempted capture—the Peruvian Government, without any doubt, has the responsibility. Of the second—the attacks on the person of Señor Salazar—I dare not, I will not, I cannot accuse that Government, because it appears to me impossible that any Government in the world would do it ; but its being done by Peruvians, and appearing to be a continuation of the other act which attaches to the said Government of Peru, there is no doubt that there is reason to call upon it to refute it on its part, and to declare its innocence by giving satisfactory explanations thereupon.

"Thus it will be said by public opinion on hearing the details of Señor Salazar ; thus it is said by the Spanish Government on hearing the statement of its Representative, which it cannot but look upon as true.

"It is not possible to hide the importance of these events from your Excellency's penetration and patriotism. They surpass those which preceded them, and they supersede them, because questions of honour take the first place amongst those nations who have a sense of honour in their hearts.

"In such a state of things your Excellency will understand what the conduct of Spain ought to be and must be who recognizes the Republic of Peru as an independent, free, and sovereign nation, but who cannot abandon without defence her citizens who reside in that country, nor permit an outrage against her Representative.

"The Spanish Government has not revindicated the Chincha Islands, nor does it think of holding them as a property belonging to it. It declares that it retains them as belonging to Peru, and that it will restore them to Peru. But it holds them now by an act of force calculated to compel that nation to administer justice to Spaniards ; and as the outrages against Señor Salazar have taken place subsequently, it will not restore them until it has received satisfaction for them, and until it is persuaded that such justice will be administered. This appears to us now to be a clear and indisputable right.

"We do not wish to humiliate Peru, nor to take away from her anything which is hers ; but, as I have said to your Excellency, we have to place our honour in safety, and we cannot abandon either the rights or the interests of the nation. We have asked for nothing, we shall ask for nothing, which should humble or degrade that state. In disapproving the conduct of its agents who endeavoured to capture the Secretary of the Spanish representative,—in declaring that it had nothing to do with the criminal attempts made against the latter, and that it is ready to exact punishment for them,—in receiving a Commissioner charged to act ("gestionar") for administering justice on the crimes of Talambo,— in nothing of this can there be any more than a fulfilment of the obligations incumbent on all of us by reason and justice. That is what we shall demand. We, on our part, as soon as those satisfactions are given to us which are required by our rights and our dignity, in that same instant we shall deliver up the Chincha Islands to the Commissioner who shall be nominated by the Government of Peru to receive them.

" We hope that this will put an end to a difference unpleasant to us, which we have not sought, which we do not exaggerate, but in which we cannot yield what our honour will not allow us to yield. We had a right to send a Representative to Lima, and the Government there had no right to refuse to receive him. We have a right to demand satisfaction for the attempts to which our Representative was near falling a victim. In the error which that Representative and Admiral Pinzon committed, expressing ideas which were not those of Her Majesty's Government, I have made no hesitation to disapprove of them: before I knew they had taken possession of the Chincha Islands I protested against the idea of revindicating or of wishing to acquire territory; after becoming acquainted with their acts I made the same protest with equal frankness, with equal precision.

" Let not our ideas, then, be misrepresented; let not our words be forgotten; let not the basis of our conduct be misunderstood. What we demand is that which we ought to demand, that which, with God's help, we are determined to maintain, that which we cannot persuade ourselves that a civilized nation like Peru will refuse to us.

" May this explanation serve your Excellency to enlighten your judgment, as also to be a rule and a guide in your relations to the Government of Her Britannic Majesty to which you are accredited, to which you may give a copy of this despatch.
" God preserve, &c.
" J. F. PACHECO."

II.

In order that my readers may form an idea of the effect produced among the South American Republics by the act committed against Peru, and the motives put forward as a justification for the seizure of the Chinchas by the Spanish Officials, I append a few translations of circulars to which the occasion gave rise, and which I arrange in the order of their date.

" Argentine Legation in Chili.
" *Valparaiso, May* 1, 1864.

" The Undersigned, Minister Plenipotentiary of the Argentine Republic, accredited to the Republic of Peru, according to the authentic copy of the credentials which he has the honour to inclose, hastens to make his appointment known to his Excellency, induced by the serious nature of the circumstances, in order to make his adhesion to the protest which the foreign Diplomatic body drew up on the 21st April last, in consequence of the violent occupation of the Chincha Islands by Spanish forces, and the unusual principles upon which it is pretended to give fair appearance to an act, the object and form of which are not in accordance with the practice of civilized nations.

"The Republics of South America belong to the community of Christian nations which governs itself by international law; they exist by their own right, which they themselves have conquered, as proved by history, and secured by universal concurrence; whilst the people from whom they have severed themselves can in no manner deny their existence, by urging the absence of Treaties or of explicit acknowledgment after forty years renunciation of all pretension of dominion, and a virtual approval of the Treaties of Ayacucho, which put an end to the war between the metropolis and its former colonies.

"The act consummated by Spanish forces at the Chincha Islands without any of the formalities which precede a declaration of hostilities between nations, endangers the peace of the greater part of the South American States, by delivering them up to the unforeseen hazards which would arise from any toleration of that ignorance of the principles of the law of nations, which the servants of the Crown of Spain proclaim with reference to a portion of the Peruvian territory.

"The undersigned therefore, awaiting instructions for his future conduct, for which he has applied to his Government, fulfils a duty belonging to his commission, and does himself honour by inscribing the name of the Argentine Republic amongst those of the States which, through their Ministers Plenipotentiary, have protested against the unusual doctrines and unlawful acts which make the armed occupation of the Chincha Islands by Spanish forces a scandalous exception to those practices and laws which govern the civilized world. At the same time, in his own name, and in that of the Argentine people, the undersigned accompanies the Government of Peru in the just indignation produced by such unjustifiable proceedings.

"The undersigned, &c.

"(*signed*) D. F. SARMIENTO.

"Legation of the United States of Colombia,
"*Valparaiso, May 3rd*, 1864.

"Sir,
"The undersigned was yesterday preparing to embark for Lima, which city he had for a time quitted, when, by reason of grave unforeseen events, he finds himself detained for 15 days

more, and for a like period delayed the day for reassuming the exercise of his functions as Envoy Extraordinary and Minister Plenipotentiary of the United States of Colombia to the Government of your Excellency.

"Above all, the undersigned was proposing immediately to adhere to the Declaration made on the 20th of April last by the Diplomatic Body, to which he has the honour to belong, in consequence of the unheard-of outrage committed by the Spanish squadron, denominated "scientific commission," which is under the orders of Admiral Pinzon and the Envoy Mazarredo, by occupying the Chincha Islands, belonging to the Republic of Peru, without previous declaration of war, and not even as a security or pledge for the payment of preferred claims.

"If we may judge by the Declaration of MM. Pinzon and Mazarredo, in which they set forth the grounds for that act of depredation, they proceed in virtue of the right of "revindication" of a property belonging to the Crown of Spain, inasmuch as the war between Spain and Peru was interrupted only by a *de facto* truce of forty years, counting from the memorable 9th of December, 1824. It is scarcely credible that the insane occupation of Peruvian territory, and the still more insane ground upon which it is sustained, can have been dictated by the Government of a nation which calls itself civilized, and which not long ago claimed to figure amongst nations of the first rank. But, on the other hand, it is not less difficult to suppose that agents selected by the Spanish Government for a special and important Commission, whatever it be, would dare in so decided a manner to exceed their instructions.

"Until in possession of other data we must reason upon the last supposition.

"Spain invades Peru without previous declaration of war, as a simple continuation of that which the world had looked upon as concluded, and as recovery of property which all nations recognise as belonging to the Peruvian Republic, to a Republic as independent as any one of themselves.

"In such a manifestation one is at a loss which most to admire, its audacity, or its imprudence. Any one might say that Spain coolly and deliberately confident in her power, and in a right derived we know not whence, comes and knocks at the door of each of its former colonies, now nations of long existence, to give them notice, foolishly and stupidly, that she undertakes the reconquest of possessions which were, but which have for ever ceased to be hers.

"Colombia, most excellent Sir, like Peru, is one of these Republics, which by their own fault have not been recognised by Spain, and to which with equal force may be applied the declaration and argument of the Spanish agents.

"Nor has Colombia been willing to purchase an independence which the arms and blood of its best sons have gained in innumerable combats, and which the names of Torres and of Caldas, of Jirardot, and of Ricaurte, of thousands and thousands more, defend by their own virtue.

"Consequently, the undersigned has conceived it to be his duty, not merely to adhere to the declaration made by his honourable colleagues. He firmly believes that his Government, and the noble people over which that Government presides, will consider the cause of Peru to be its own in the present emergency, and in every other one of the kind. He thinks, and in so thinking he fears not to differ from that Government and from that people, that the alarm of Spain at the Chinchas will not sound in vain for Colombia; that, heard throughout her mountains and valleys, it will raise, armed for combat, the old and young, the rich and the poor, all classes and all parties.

"For, if Spain, as it would seem, has learnt nothing during her truce of forty years, America, her former slave, has raised herself to the rank of Sovereign; has cultivated relations with really civilized nations; has tasted, even amidst disturbances, the sweets of liberty; has drawn morality from sources purer than those known to Cortes and to Pizarro, to Pinzon and to Mazarredo; has shaken off the absurd fanaticism of Philip II. and of Torquemada; has acquired a true notion of political and social economy; has broken the chains of the slave; and, finally, has learnt to exist without her former master, whose obstinate and proud moroseness has been a constant matter of amazement for her better instructed descendants.

"Although the Government of your Excellency cannot doubt the sentiments and purposes of the Colombian Union in the crisis which Peru is going through for her own glory, the undersigned has been unable to resist the desire here to interpret them, in like manner as he desires, very earnestly, that your Excellency will accept, &c.

(*signed*) " JUSTO AROSEMENA."

CIRCULAR ADDRESSED BY THE CHILIAN MINISTER FOR FOREIGN AFFAIRS, TO THE AMERICAN GOVERNMENTS.

"*Santiago, May 4th*, 1864.

"SIR,

"The occupation of the Chincha Islands by the naval forces of Spain in the Pacific, has caused in the mind of the Chilian Government the most profound and painful impression, and awakened in all the Republic a lively alarm, which will be equally felt from one extremity to the other of the American continent.

"Her Catholic Majesty's Commissary and the Commander-in-chief of the squadron in the Pacific, under whose personal responsibility this act appears to have been perpetrated, are not unaware of its gravity, and they have endeavoured to justify it, setting forth, in the declaration issued from the anchorage at the Chincha Islands, the motives which had decided them to take that resolution.

"If this measure be considered as reprisals, calculated to obtain reparation for some injury or offence proffered to Spain by Peru, it is necessary to inquire if the moment had arrived to appeal to an almost extreme resource, when the pacific measures employed by nations to avoid the calamities of war were not exhausted.

"The right which Sovereign States ascribe to themselves to obtain justice, is marked by certain proceedings, which the constant practice of nations has constituted as tutelary principles of the peace and harmony upon which the common welfare of societies is based. To deviate from them without a just motive is an offence, which not only affects the interests of the State to which it is proffered, but also involves a general deviation from those general and obligatory rules, in the faithful observance of which all the members of the great family of sovereign and independent nations should interest themselves.

"The declaration set forth by the Commissary of Her Catholic Majesty, and by the Commander-in-Chief of her squadron in the Pacific, besides being liable to a just censure, viewed in the light which has been indicated, is neither more nor less than the sanction of principles which place in doubt the independence of Peru, and provoke a conflict throughout all America.

"Thus, the Government of Chili cannot do otherwise than to reprobate, as it does most explicitly, such doctrines, and to protest against them, although confident that they will not be sanctioned by the Government of Her Catholic Majesty.

"The independence of Peru, and its existence as a free and Sovereign State, is a fact not to be disputed, and even to doubt this it would be necessary to obliterate the history of half-a-century, converting into a simple truce what in reality has been a durable and indefinite peace, universally accepted, and acknowledged by Spain herself in a long series of public and official acts. The Government of Her Catholic Majesty for many years has invariably styled "Republic" that which formerly was her colony. This is repeated in the credentials of the Commissary, which she has just sent to Lima; she has received the Consuls of the Republic and allowed its ships to frequent the ports of the Peninsula, and between the two countries a reciprocal commerce has been maintained without interruption; lastly, she has considered the Peruvians as foreigners in the Peninsula, in the same manner as the Spaniards are looked upon as foreigners in Peru. As a Sovereign State, Peru has negotiated Treaties of Peace, Friendship and Commerce with nations of both Continents; and with these facts before us, known to the Government of Her Catholic Majesty, can any force be attached, in the face of truth and the law of nations, to the want of a formal recognition, so as to found upon this a state of truce?

"A truce supposes no communication, and it may even be said that this is its characteristic; nor is a long and indefinite armistice ended without a previous declaration of the intention to renew hostilities, an essential formality set forth by the practice of ancient and modern nations.

"According to the judgment of the Commissary of Her Catholic Majesty and the Commander-in-Chief of the Pacific, the Crown of Castille is in a position to recover the dominion of the Chincha Islands, and appears to derive this right as a logical consequence of the supposed truce. A nation constituted for forty years, exercising independently acts of sovereignty throughout all the extension of its territory, is not, nor can be, subject to a demand of recovery. The taking possession of the Chincha Islands by the Spanish squadron becomes, in such a case, an act brought about by force, and is destitute of all the requisites which constitute a legitimate act; the right of recovery would become a right of reconquest.

"The armies of Chili fought side by side with those of Peru in the war of independence; the two Republics were one and the same in a common cause, as were also the other sections of America. Hostilities being renewed, there having been only a truce, what is the situation in which the old belligerents of all the Continent and their Allies are forcibly placed?

"In view of so grave an event, it is the rigorous duty of the Government of Chili to reject, in the most public and solemn manner, the principles which form the bases of the declaration, and protest against the occupation of the Chincha Islands by the naval forces of Her Catholic Majesty, and it does not acknowledge, nor will it acknowledge, as legitimate owner of those Islands, any other Power than the Republic of Peru.

"It entertains, however, the conviction that the Government of Her Catholic Majesty will not accept nor approve of the principles proclaimed in that declaration, because, if the principle of recovery were sanctioned, the Republics of America would find themselves called upon by duty to combine their forces in order to maintain the integrity of an independent sister Republic.

"It would be painful if the rapid and inevitable development of events should bring about complications, either by retarding the conclusion of an international question, to which the Government of Peru is disposed to lend due attention in order to arrange in a firm and permanent manner their differences with Spain, or by preparing new difficulties which considerations of a superior order would render necessary to be opportunely avoided by the Government of America.

"The manifestation which I have now set forth, in compliance with the orders which I have received from the President of the

Republic, will be considered, I hope, by the Government of your Excellency, as the faithful expression of the general sentiments of all America.

"The Government of ———— abounding in the same sentiments will, I doubt not, be pleased to learn the views of Chili, and the disposition in which she finds herself to act in conjunction to avoid a conflict which may disturb the peace of this Continent by interrupting the friendly relations which happily she has cultivated, and desires to cultivate with the Spanish nation.

"I have, &c.,

(*signed*) "MANUEL ANTO. TOCORNAL."

"*Caracas, May* 28*th*, 1864.

"EXCELLENCY,

"The Government of the United States of Venezuela has attentively read your Excellency's despatch of the 26th of April, conveying the information of the unlooked for despoliation of the Chincha Islands suffered by Peru, at the hands of the Spanish squadron in the Pacific, without any previous declaration of war. Your Excellency's note, that of the Venezuelan Plenipotentiary resident in Lima, and the documents sent by that diplomatist, have placed my Government in possession of all the necessary antecedents to form a clear opinion of the events, and to enable it to express its intentions relative to their future development.

"First of all, the Venezuelan Government sympathises with that of Peru in the defence of her property seized so greatly in opposition to the civilization of the age; for whatever be the motives of complaint which Spain entertains against your Excellency's Government, the Representatives of Her Catholic Majesty could not consider themselves exempted from the forms which the law of nations has consecrated in favour of the world's peace, and of the confraternity of its inhabitants, as a guarantee to the weak, and a barrier to the powerful.

"No doubt it was to remove the universal condemnation of the non-compliance with international usage, that the right of dominion was appealed to by Spain over the Islands she has seized under the pretence that no explicit recognition of the independence of Peru existed on the part of the mother-country. But it cannot be admitted that the right of dominion can be imprescriptible for ever; this is the opinion of my Government; to admit such a right would be equivalent to a deprivation of the right appertaining to all the peoples of the world to assume their sovereignty, and to inscribe their names amongst nations.

"In the case of Peru, forty years of independence undisputed by Spain, her recognition by the Governments of Europe and America, and the diplomatic and other intercourse carried on by Spain herself with her former colony as between State and State, for a long interval of time, are sufficient to uphold that the independence of the Peruvian nation is a positive fact, and consequently to impugn the pretension put forward that the occupation of the Chincha Islands, an integral part of the territory of that Republic, is considered as a continuation of the war of independence in America. In the opinion of the Venezuelan Government, that war terminated *de facto* at the surrender of Callao in 1826, and it also ended by right, since Spain admitted Peru in its relations as a sovereign nation, recognising in this implicit manner that she was irrevocably separated from the Peninsular dominion.

"From all these precedents, the necessary consequence to be deduced is, that Señor Salazar y Mazarredo and Admiral Pinzon have violated, without any justifiable reasons, the sovereignty of Peru, and wounded the honour of America, the people and Government of which are by the nature of their institutions, history, and civilization, united in the preservation of their prerogatives.

"My Government, nevertheless, entertains the hope expressed by your Excellency, that the Government of Madrid will disapprove the conduct of their Commissary and of the Commander of the Spanish squadron, and will renew their diplomatic intercourse with Peru, so as to arrive at a pacific understanding honourable to both Powers. But, if contrary to all expectation and considerations of justice, our hopes should prove fallacious, and the Government of Her Catholic Majesty should accept the responsibility of the acts of their Representatives, Venezuela will consider herself authorized to suspect, in view of such serious facts, that the designs of dominion over America attributed to certain European powers, are not an unfounded supposition, and to believe that it is time to look out for her own independence, declaring from the present moment, as my Government does declare, that she will not sever the unity which binds her as an American and Republican Government to the other Republics of this Continent, for the defence which they may be called upon to make of their autonomy and institutions.

"The President of the United States of Venezuela, in giving me instructions to reply to your Excellency in the manner I have done, has directed me also to state, that a copy of this note will be transmitted to the Diplomatic agents of Venezuela accredited to sundry Governments; and directly to those of America where there are no agents, so that the attitude assumed by the Venezuelan nation in consequence of the violent despoliation suffered by Peru, may be generally and officially known, and that it may serve them as a guide in every instance when the nature of events does not permit them to obtain special instructions.

"The Undersigned, &c.

(*signed*) "J. G. Ochoa."

III.

THE CHINCHA ISLANDS.

Their importance to Peru.

A few words respecting these Islands will not perhaps be deemed superfluous.

They are situated in the Bay of Pisco, on the coast of Peru, in Lat. 13° 38′ S. and Long. 76° 12′ W. and are about 120 miles to the North of Lima. They consist of a group of three naked rocks, lying in a line from North to South, each of about two miles circumference, presenting the form of flattened cones, and on the eastern side a perpendicular wall of rock. From the craggy edge of this wall, Huano or Guano, as it is indifferently called—being the accumulation of the excrement of millions of sea-birds, (pelicans, gannets, mews, mutton birds, divers, gulls, penguins &c.) formed during thousands of years,—slopes towards the middle of each Island, where a pinnacle of rock rises above the surface, whence there is a gentle slope to the western shores, with Guano to within a few feet of the water.

The ancient Peruvians, there is no doubt, used the Guano as a manure, and under the Incas it would appear that very severe laws secured the birds from being disturbed during the hatching season at these Islands. When the Spaniards took possession of Peru, the Chinchas fell into desuetude, but although unused, it cannot be ascertained whether the deposits of Guano have increased during the subsequent 300 years.

These deposits of Guano have been formally declared the property of the State, and the Peruvian Government authorities have, since 1840, made them a source of revenue of yearly increasing importance.

The revenue derived from them forms the security for the payment of interest and capital of the public debts which Peru has contracted, more especially in England. In 1859, the revenue derived from Guano, amounted to . . . $15,875,352
From Customs, to 3,391,342
And from all other sources, including a balance of nearly a million from the previous year, only 1,688,097

Making together $20,954,791

To meet an expenditure of $20,387,756

This shows at a glance the importance of these Islands to Peru, and, I may add, to her creditors.

From the beginning of 1841 to the end of 1860, that is to say, in 20 years, Peru exported 3,220,939 tons register, equal to more than 4,000,000 tons weight of Guano; by which the Government is estimated to have realized net proceeds to the amount of above £20,000,000 sterling.

In September, 1853, the Government sent a Commission of Engineers and Naturalists to the Chincha Inlands to ascertain as accurately as the case admitted, the amount of Guano still existing on the Chincha Islands.

The surveys of these gentlemen go to prove that the deposits,

On the Northern Island were about	4,189,477 effective tons.
On the Middle Island	2,505,948
On the Southern Island	5,680,695
Together,	12,376,100 tons.

The Chinchas are popularly called the Guano Islands, from the circumstance of the Guano having been hitherto drawn from them; but Peru possesses some others further north, the Guano deposits of which were surveyed and measured last year, with the following results, as published in "El Comercio" of Lima on the 13th June, 1863.

	Tons.					Estimated net proceeds.
Lobos Islands (two)	3,000,000,	1st class,	£6	per ton		£18,000,000
Do.	1,000,000	2nd	„	4	„	4,000,000
Macabi Islands (two)	1,500,000	1	„	6	„	9,000,000
Guañapa Islands	2,500,000	1	„	6	„	15,000,000
Not less than	8,000,000 tons.					£46,000,000

Add the deposits of the Chincha Islands, making an allowance for the exports between 1858 and 1863, six years, and reducing it to, say (11,000,000 tons) at £6.	£66,000,000
And we obtain a total from this source of	£112,000,000

THE END.

www.ingramcontent.com/pod-product-compliance
Lightning Source LLC
Chambersburg PA
CBHW020231090426
42735CB00010B/1647